Ji — Never give up hope,

Judy Hindy

Losing Is NOT an Option

LOSING IS NOT AN OPTION
Life Lessons from a Baseball Mom

JUDY HINDY, RN, MSN

XULON PRESS

Xulon Press
2301 Lucien Way #415
Maitland, FL 32751
407.339.4217
www.xulonpress.com

© 2019 by Judy Hindy, RN, MSN

All rights reserved solely by the author. The author guarantees all contents are original and do not infringe upon the legal rights of any other person or work. No part of this book may be reproduced in any form without the permission of the author. The views expressed in this book are not necessarily those of the publisher.

Unless otherwise indicated, Scripture quotations taken from the Holy Bible, New International Version (NIV). Copyright © 1973, 1978, 1984, 2011 by Biblica, Inc.™. Used by permission. All rights reserved.

Printed in the United States of America.

ISBN-13: 978-1-54565-907-6

About the Author

Judy Hindy, RN MSN has worked in the hospital setting in various positions for over 30 years. She has extensive and diverse experience working as a Unit Secretary, Human Resource Assistant in Nursing Recruitment, Nurse Technician, Registered Nurse, and Clinical Nurse Educator. She is also a wife and mother of three boys, two in college and one in high school. In 2015, Judy was diagnosed with metastatic colon cancer and had to quit her job and undergo aggressive chemotherapy treatment, colon resection, liver wedge resection, and is still under treatment. She remains hopeful that she can get to remission and return to a position in the health care industry to help others with their health care needs.

About the Book

Judy Hindy, with her over 30 years of hospital experience, and, watching her kids play baseball, found many similarities of people's every day struggles. She wrote this book to help others understand life's journey is just like a baseball game. You win some, lose some, but you must always "keep your head in the game," because "losing is not an option." She walks you through the many life lessons players learn in the game and people learn to deal with in life. This book helps the reader find ways to get through those trials with a positive approach. She uses real life stories of players who have struggled with fears, frustrations, failures, getting along with difficult people, and so many other life issues in order to discover that you are not alone. Each chapter will leave you inspired, learn new coping skills, and give you new hope until the very end when you finally realize the most valuable life lesson, of never giving up.

Table of Contents

About the Author................................vii
About the Book..................................ix
Preface xiii

1. Opening Day.................................. 1
2. What Makes a Great Coach?..................... 5
3. Friendship................................... 11
4. It's not even the first inning and some people
   bail out 19
5. It's NOT a ONE MAN Game.................... 23
6. Rocked on the Mound........................ 25
7. Step Up to the Plate 27
8. Just Let it Go............................... 33
9. Hitting a Wall 39
10. When the Going Gets Tough, Get Going 47
11. Accountability.............................. 51

12. Fear 55
13. Hurting the Team 59
14. Bad Attitude 63
15. Underachievement 67
16. Dealing with Difficult People 73
17. Taking Your Share of Lumps 77
18. Out of Control 81
19. Cancer Destroys a Team 89
20. Losing the Big Game 97
21. Knowing when you're on a losing team 99
22. Pressing On but Live in the Moment 103
23. The Game is Not Over 107
24. The Season is Over 111
25. Saying Goodbye 115
26. Starting Over 119
27. Never Stop Fighting...Losing Is Not an Option...Keep Your Head in the Game 123

Preface

I give God the Glory in everything I've learned in life. Life is like a baseball game, there are only so many innings, some go strong, inning after inning, some sit on the bench, and some don't even play at all. I have played the game of life strong and hard throughout the years. I have learned that I cannot do it alone. I need to honor God, allow Him to lead me each step of the way, and never step out of the batter's box, no matter what comes over the plate. Many people chose to find their own way, make up the rules as they go along, and live as if they are the center of the universe. That may work for a while, but I've found that when life sends you a curve ball, it's a game changer. I have given my life to Jesus Christ, even when I was a little child and my faith grew over the years but, it was never all that simple or easy. There were times I totally forgot about Christ and did it my way, only to find myself in a big mess. I realized quickly that I needed a foundation, a relationship with someone who truly loved me, and a purpose bigger than myself. It's when I allowed God to lead the way, I started my journey to a better place with a better attitude, and a more fulfilling lifestyle. This doesn't mean I didn't have struggles as we all will face sooner or later. Just like in baseball, you don't always win each game. There are games where you come out dominating and some you strike out every time you're up to bat. So, what can you do differently to make a difference? Certainly, you need to go back to the basics and come up with a new approach. For me it was with prayer. I've learned to pray for directions, answers, and strength to endure what I was facing. I had to rely on God to lead me the way, trust Him totally, and be patient. It doesn't happen overnight, nor does improving your skills, winning a game, or getting the season trophy. Just like players look to their coaches for direction, I look to God for mine. God gives me the rules that are all clearly written in the Bible. He has shown me how He loves me by dying on cross for me and my sins. Forgiveness is no light matter, when I have messed up on so many occasions. The hardest thing was to learn to forgive myself, but He did it all for me. All He asked me was to let Him be the center of my world. He gave us only two commandments, to love Him and to love others. So I've learned to trust Him with my life, give Him all the glory, and let Him be my head coach. Many players try to do it on their own and fail big time. I've done that throughout my life, when I forgot about asking God for direction. I've just seen God throughout my life do miracles, but you don't always see these miracles until you're willing and when the darkness turns to light. When I was a little girl, I

Preface

asked God to help my mother, who was being abused by my dad. I asked Him to protect her from him because she was a good woman who loved her kids and did her best to raise all six of us, with a ninth-grade education. Well, my dad eventually left and we had peace, but were in a financial dilemma. I had to put my dreams of going to nursing school on the backburner and work full-time to support my family. Then the most heart-wrenching disease struck my mom, as she was diagnosed with metastatic breast cancer. By God's grace, I was able to put her on my health care insurance, along with my two younger siblings, to assists us with her medical bills. I believe this was God helping our family but didn't see this miracle at the time. The only thing I felt was darkness, fatigue, and frustration trying to work full-time, go to college, and care for my mom who was paralyzed from waist down from the tumor in her spine. Fortunately, I was able to come home during lunch to assist her with her needs, which was another blessing from God. We also needed someone to care for her during the day, so my aunt came to help. This was a special miracle from God, because my aunt was such a good cook and we always had meals when we got home from work. We cared for my mom for two years before she passed away but we had many funny stories, spent special times, and loved her until the very end. I hit rock bottom of depression after this because not only did my mom die, my boyfriend broke up with me, and my job was going nowhere. Again, God showed up one day, walking around the track as I saw this light beam into my eyes and heart.

It was powerful, warm, and I heard a soft voice whisper into my ears that it was time to go to nursing school. I didn't believe this and had no clue how I was going to fulfill this goal, considering I had no confidence, no money, and no time to do this. Except, something burned inside of me that moved me into action. I asked God to come into my life again, to lead me the way. I went to church often, but this time I prayed harder than ever before. I knelt down and asked God to help me to accomplish this dream I've had since I was a teenager but, didn't know how it would be possible. Well, I've learned that all things are possible with God and He was with me each step of the way. Again, it wasn't easy, I took a part-time job while going to school and every day I kept praying for God to get me through each test, each class, and each semester. Well after thirteen years of working and going to school, I graduated with my Bachelor of Science in Nursing from the University of Detroit Mercy. The irony of this is just ten years prior I walked on this campus with my mom and my sister wanting to go to this school but couldn't at the time. Well, God had a plan for me, but it just took a little longer than what I thought was possible. That is why I'm a firm believer to never give up on your dreams, give it to God, and allow God to lead you the way. Sometimes, God has a different plan than you do but, you have to trust Him, that He knows what is best. I believe that I achieved my goal through much pain and hard work, which allowed me to value what I accomplished. This gave me a new passion for helping others and it was that which guided me in

Preface

my profession every day. The best part of all of this, was I found a Godly man, one year prior to graduation. I asked God during my mom's illness, to help me find a man who would lead me to a stronger relationship with Him. I wanted a man who loved God as much as I did and would raise our kids in the Christian faith. Well, just after my mom passed away, my head nurse asked me if I would meet a guy she knew through a friend of hers on a blind date. I thought she was crazy, but I had nothing else to lose after having a failed relationship. When I met this man, I realized there was something different about him. He was genuine, kind, had a sense of humor, his car was spotless, and he was a Christian. It didn't take long before I knew this was who God sent me and, twenty-three years together, I believe God sent him to me for a reason. We have three amazing boys, who I love with all my heart. They have also accepted Jesus Christ in their lives, which has given me such peace and joy. I loved being a mother, wife, nurse, and witness to others through our lives. People think being a Christian, you have to live a perfect life, far from that. We all sin and only God is perfect. Yes, even I can be a pistol, selfish, and forget about what God teaches me in the Bible. Thankfully, for grace, the grace God has given me, the grace my husband gives me, and the grace I give to myself and others is what allows me to grow stronger in faith. I have a great church that supports me in the word, fellowship, and activities to keep our family strong. We may mess up during the week, but come Sunday, it reminds us where we went wrong, shows us what we need to focus on, and we leave with a full tank of gas. Sometimes, you just have to allow God to work in your life, but first you have to come to Him humbly and admit you need Him in your life. I've learned throughout the years of my marriage, raising three boys, that it's not easy, but the most powerful lesson God has taught me is "Losing Is Not an Option" with Him. I truly believe that no matter where life takes you on the journey, if you have a personal relationship with Jesus Christ, you will not go wrong. He will open your eyes to the beautiful nature and all the Blessings life can provide. I couldn't see those blessings during those difficult challenges because I was so stressed, but looking back at my life, I see the hand of God holding me up, giving me a way out, and showing me unconditional love. My family is the most important part of my life and is the most precious blessing I have received. Raising boys has brought me to my knees praying for them to become men of honor, like their father. My family has faced many obstacles over the years, but we face them with the help of God. The most difficult challenge we faced, was when I was diagnosed with metastatic colon cancer. This rocked our world and brought us to our knees. This was a time in our lives where everything was going good. I completed my masters in nursing education and was working as a Clinical Nurse Educator and a nurse in the Intensive Care Unit. My husband continued his job as a physician in a family practice office. We are very active in our church and community, so this took everyone by surprise. One thing you will discover is that we are most involved

Preface

in our kids' baseball programs. All three boys played baseball at one time, but it was my son Joseph who made it his passion to continue on throughout many challenging years. We'd just got back from a fantastic vacation in Myrtle Beach, for the Cal Ripken baseball tournament Joe played in. We had the time of our lives competing with teams from around the world; we even played a team from Australia. I was scheduled for a routine colonoscopy that August, when the doctor found a tumor so large, she couldn't pass a pediatric scope through it. Then the CT Scan confirmed that it had spread throughout my body, to my liver and lymph nodes. Here I am facing life and death with three young boys. Joseph was in his senior year in high school and was looking at options to play in college. Thomas was still playing high school baseball and travel baseball, and Joshua was in middle school, who decided to turn in his bat and glove just after T-ball. When a person faces challenges, it brings you to your knees and makes you discover a whole new meaning of life's importance. I had to immediately quit my two jobs and enter an aggressive chemotherapy treatment regimen. Our family faced this together, with turning to God for help. We all prayed together in our living room, but God gave us strength, hope, and peace. This was not going to be an easy journey for nothing was certain, and we had to rely on our faith. We knew that no matter what happened, that I loved the Lord with all my heart and so did my family. We depended on God, our family, our church, and our community for support. Every day I went for my treatment I relied on God more than ever.

The regimen was brutal and left me in tears so many days. I was sick, I was weak, I lost twenty pounds, and I was afraid that I wouldn't make it. I endured a colon resection, liver wedge resection, radiation, and chemotherapy, over a three-year period. By the grace of God, I'm still going strong, even though I'm still receiving additional chemotherapy treatment in hopes of remission. I asked God to allow me to see my son graduate, and now both my boys have graduated and are in college, Joshua is a freshman in high school, and I am still unable to work as a nurse. As a family, we are still very active in our church, school, and community. We are still a baseball family but, are now even enjoying the beauty of music as Joshua is playing the trumpet in the band at school. He is quite a talented musician, who also plays in our church band the trumpet and the bassoon. He loves music and wants to take it to the college level. My son Thomas is in college in a Biomedical Engineering Program with a dream to become an Orthopedic Surgeon. He continues to play baseball on a travel team but chose not to play at the college level. However, Joseph made it to the college level and is one of the reasons I wrote this book. Throughout the years watching my boys play baseball, I've learned many valuable life lessons along the way. I wasn't just sitting in the stands rooting for my kid and his team but observing everything and everyone in the game. I've used many of these life lessons to help me through my cancer journey. The lessons I've learned have been an eye opener on how ridiculous we can be at times, when we don't have a core

Preface

belief in other than ourselves. I've chosen to live my life to love God with all my heart and soul, and to love others, but not everyone believes as I do. What I have observed are players and people in life have to figure things out by themselves, in their own time frame, and with their own moral compass. For me, life had more meaning with God in my life because I didn't have to rely on myself to figure it all out. Life can be complicated for many people, as it brings on many challenges. Over the years I saw a parallel between life and each game my son played. I've learned through all of this that you have a choice, to keep your head in the game or bail out. You will win some games and lose others; you may be the best player or the worst. The one thing that I taught my son is to never give up. No matter what the game throws at you, no matter how hard it gets, no matter how many bad calls, bad plays, bad outcomes, you keep giving it your all. I did this with my cancer journey and am still going strong by the grace of God. The most important thing I want my boys to learn is not to quit. It's easy to sit on the bench of life and watch it pass you buy. It's easy to take the shorter road, lie, cheat, steal, or don't even care about the future of the game or of life. But it takes courage, commitment, and character to stand up for what you believe in. It takes a heart that believes in the possibility to make things happen. It takes faith to step out of your comfort zone, to do things that you wouldn't think possible. I watched all three of my boys throughout their lives make this the foundation to build on. I've watched them struggle, pour their hearts out, and give all they have for where they are now in their lives. I watched them give to others around them with kindness, friendship, and love. They have served within our church, school, and community to give back to others. I'm proud of everything they have become, especially with their walk with our Christian faith. I'm proud of their father for leading them along the way with being a role model of Christ. He has been patient, kind, gentle, and loving to me and our boys. He gives so much of himself to his family, church, patients, and services in our community. It's not all about what you get in life, but what you can give back. It's believing in the impossible and stepping up to the plate to make it happen. Nothing happens when you sit on the sidelines, you just get weaker. It takes a commitment to give your talents to a team, to make everyone better around you. It's not all about you, but the team. So many people go through life thinking it's all about them when in reality, the best part of life is what you do to make the team around you stronger. Whether it's on your job, in your family, or on a baseball team, you can make life better for yourself while helping others along the way. The most important life lesson I can stress to my sons is that you may get down, you may even fail, but you never quit the game of baseball or of life. You dig down, deep within yourself, rise to the occasion, and press on. Don't ever quit when the darkness surrounds you, you continue to play the game with heart and passion until the last inning. You must always believe in the impossible because, as I always tell

Preface

everyone along the way, "Losing Is Not an Option," "Keep your Head in the Game," it's a total game changer!

Opening Day

It is opening day, sunny, and a great morning to play a game of baseball. The field is ready, players are arriving, and you can smell the food coming from the concession stand. All the kids are excited to start the season, the parents cannot wait to see their kids play, while the coaches only desire is to win. This is what they trained for even before the season started. This is the day that provides an opportunity to earn the winning trophy, but only one team will come in first place. This is what a famous coach told my son, one day, as I arrived with him on the ball field. I was a new mom to baseball and honestly, I did not know what I was going to face and learn over the next many seasons to come. I learned more about baseball from this coach than I could of if I played the game myself. Along with the game, he taught me some valuable life lessons that followed everything he preached to the kids. He had passion and the love for the game. I have not seen a person with such drive, determination, and commitment in such a long time. People wander aimlessly through life with no purpose, but he had purpose, passion, and a vision that inspired others who cared to listen. Life is not meant to live with no purpose or passion. What is the point to just exist, if not for the hope of accomplishing something meaningful? I was inspired by his constant drive for excellence and vision for success. I watched as he took players such as my son and taught them how to pitch, hit, field, and catch as beginners into a team that won the season trophy. I watched him turn my kid, who showed up with a vinyl glove and cheap bat, into an all-star player by the end of the season. You may ask how he did this; I look back and wondered the same question myself. I pondered also how can I apply this same winning spirit in my life and accomplish my dreams. I could only attribute this to everything he told the kids over the season. His words ran through my head again and again as I heard him instruct the kids. I saw the eyes of those kids as they looked to him for advice, encouragement, and some affirmation. Sometimes, coaches are the only parent who truly believes in them, and he did. He believed in their potential and used each kid's talents to gel a team that functioned as a well-oiled machine. The kids came to practice excited to learn more because someone gave them something they did not have before they came: courage. For it takes courage to face your fears, deal with your challenges, and courage to arrive at the desired destiny. That is the heartfelt lesson I learned from sitting in the dugout, for every practice and watching every game. I learned that it takes courage to take on life challenges, but when you have someone who stands with you through the hard times, nothing is impossible. Every practice was exciting and fun, as I watched my son grown along the way. He blossomed and was determined to prove to his coach that he was worthy of his time. He did not want to fail and followed everything his coach told him to do. As a mom, I was proud to be a part of something meaningful that moved me to believe that my kid could be all he could be. My kid would learn to understand not only the game of baseball, but how to grow, develop, and mature as a future man. Some kids never grow up, nor find their gifts, just to live each day as if tomorrow would never come. No, my kid knew that he had many talents and gifts that he was inspired to use in life to only take him far beyond his limited imagination. He learned that with courage, confidence, and conviction that he could face his giants in life. He learned that all from a game of baseball. His coach taught us all valuable lessons that we used for the next years to come. I applied the same principles from baseball to our family life. I was a new mom when it came to sports, but it was what I learned along the way from the game that kept me from "bailing out." Life is a baseball game and some may stay in it for an inning, while others will stay in it until the lights are turned off in the field. It is all in how you look at it and how you play the game. Although, I will never forget what his coach always said that kept me from bailing out and he was so right! You have to "keep your head in the game!" I was a proud mom after that season, to be part of a winning team and the best coach that Algonac will ever see.

What Makes a Great Coach?

Philippians 2:3 "Do nothing out of selfish ambition or vain conceit. Rather, in humility value others above yourselves" NIV

Throughout the years there have been some awesome coaches. The difference between the good ones and the not so good ones, are the ones who can lead a team. Many of the best coaches used their role to personally and professionally inspire others. Some coaches are not well paid, some volunteer their time, while others obtain a hefty salary. The hardest part of being a coach is overcoming the pressures and obstacles to prevent them from victory. Coaches endure tremendous pressure from their players, fans, other teams, umpires, administration, and their own family, who pays a great price for their dedication to the game. Despite all the hurdles that they have to overcome, many coaches stand out as mentors, role models, and as leaders. Many coaches overcome these obstacles with the vision, perseverance, and commitment to take the team to a championship. It is hard to keep your eye on that goal but a great coach is able to inspire his team to "keep their heads in the game" and not lose sight or take for granted the challenges that will lead them to victory. Others get too caught up in the moment and take their sight off the winning prize. They become disgruntled and lose heart to what it takes to create opportunities for the future of the team. While others understand that it is developing the character, heart, and souls of each player to reach beyond their limited capacities and go for the glory. The most important thing a great coach understands is that success is not about one player but a team that works together to conquer each team they face.

    The coach who can be a mentor to the team is able to reach down inside of each player to capture his or her personal best. They develop a personal and professional relationship that harbors respect, compassion, and loyalty. The coach looks out for each player's best interest in fostering open communication that will lead to honest conversations. Communication is key as a mentor because a coach must know how to reach each player to develop that personal relationship. There are times that it just pays to sit and get to know the player for who he or she is, at the core. Understanding this dimension can assist with building and shaping the goals for that player on the team. The coach wants to reach deep within each player's heart with an understanding that his or her contribution is vital to the team's success. Mentorship takes time and patience. Not all players are going to be open to the vision set forth. Time will be needed to get each player to come on board with what is at stake for the team. Some players may take longer to buy into the plan and can create many challenges for a coach to deal with as the season moves on. These players may be all about themselves and not care about the team concept. While other players are more open and accepting of what a coach demands of them. These players are able to be easily mentored, because they capture the spirit of the team concept. They are flexible, coachable, and are willing to do what it takes to follow the lead of the coach. They may enjoy the relationship fostered from the coach and motivate other team members to follow coarse too. Mentorship requires a two way relationship that involves a positive attitude, a willing spirit, and a passion for the game. A coach that is able to mentor the team to face challenges of each game will eventually develop the respect needed to bind them together to achieve success.

A great coach is also a role model. This coach should show the team that he or she has the knowledge, experience, and skills to lead the team to a winning season. A positive role model is a person who leads by example. Nothing is truer than to show the courage, strength, and character in fostering a team approach. Being a role model is vital to the team's success because the team looks to the coach for leadership. Coaches must make some of the toughest decisions and show they have it all together, even when the game is out of control. Many coaches fall apart and so does the team, when faced with a challenging game. The game then becomes a part of their personal goals and forget it is about the whole team. They forget that being a role model is to exemplify the character required during each game. Challenges is just what makes the game exciting and facing each challenge with the right approach teaches the team exactly what you are made of. Being a role model is no easy task, because everyone has their personal flaws, but owning up to those flaws are what defines you as a great role model. Nobody expects a coach to be perfect, but honest enough to know their inner strengths and weaknesses that can interfere with the success of the team. You face those challenges together and with the love and support of the team. A great coach doesn't have to prove his or herself but just leads by example. Their character is such that each player looks up to them for direction and follows in their footsteps. A great coach can inspire others in being a role model in leading the team throughout the season.

Most importantly, a great coach has to be a great leader. A coach has to command authority, yet to be fair, and impartial. No coach is justified in making decisions that do not support the team. The coach cannot show favoritism to one player over another without justification. His or her decision to give some players more time on the field is based upon sound reasoning and always puts the team's best interest at heart. There are going to be many outcomes that coaches do not like, agree with, or may tolerate. This does not give coaches the right to make players suffer for the poor decisions they have made. Instead, they need to be responsible for what happens on and off the field. The coach can be a leader by setting the tone, providing clear rules, and providing the vision for positive outcomes. This leader cannot be judgmental, too critical, or push their players beyond reasonable expectations. They need to be realistic in their approach with the level of skills on the team and know how to unify it in achieving each win. This is how a great leader can earn respect and foster a winning spirit within the team. Leadership is all about attitude and approach, with creating positive changes that lead to productive outcomes. Coaches can be great leaders in making monumental moments seem so easy. Great leadership takes the courage, confidence, and conviction to stand strong among the weak and press on toward the goal. This is what makes teams win championships and what makes them remembered for a lifetime.

Friendship

John 15:13 "Greater love has no one than this that he lay down his life for his friends" **John 15:17** "This is my command: Love each other" NIV

A team must rely on strong friendships to strengthen the foundation it stands on. A team must develop trust, unity, and friendship, to develop over the season. Players spend so much time with each other, they develop a bond. A brotherhood creates a character of the team that reflects what each player is made of. Brotherhood means believing in each other, caring for each other, and building each other up even through the most challenging games. It relies on strength, courage, and commitment to each other. Team players must be dependable, honest, and trustworthy to make it through the challenges of each game. Discouragement, mistakes, and failures are a reality when a team hits the field. Friendship can be a game changer when a team can uplift each other, focus on the positives, and push each other through the barriers faced. No one is going to agree on everything or become the best of friends at times, but for the team to succeed, friendship is part of what separates the winners from the losers. A team relies on developing a positive relationship of players who bring their talents, time, and tributes to build upon. Each player contributes their absolute best with a positive attitude, uplifting spirit, and commitment to have each other's backs. The game cannot rely on a one man team to succeed, but a unit of players. This unit is focused on working together as a group of individuals who are willing to risk it all for the prize. This friendship is celebrated during the season through many victories, strengthened during many challenges, and remains even stronger, as the team progresses through the season to the very end. No matter if the team wins or loses, friendship will be celebrated and keep each player's head in the game. At the end of the season, it will be the friends that made a difference and never be forgotten. For it is the friendships that push you to be the best you can be in and out of the game, because they are the people who truly believe in you and will go the distance with you!

Friendship can be so difficult to find, maintained, and given to others. For some people are concerned with what they receive rather than what they give. These people consume others with their needs, wants, and demands. They are selfish, arrogant, and manipulative. Still others are not focused about what they get in return. Many times, those two types develop friendships and it ends bitterly. It is a give and take relationship of two people whose focus is on building a bond of trust, honesty, and commitment. A friend is someone who is willing to walk beside you, even in the darkest moment, not leaving when it gets tough, but stays the course until the end. A friend is someone who is willing to build you up by believing in you. This friend can see things that you may not see in yourself, but shows you your true worth. A friend is willing to take a risk to have those courageous conversations, take the time needed, and push you to be the best you can be. A friend listens, understands, and has enormous patience to see you through the storms in life. This friend is willing to be there to lift you up when you fail. Yet, a friend is someone who will celebrate your victories. Friendship is not always easy and, at times, taken for granted even between the best of friends. You have to be willing to take on such a challenge and this takes a special person inside and out.

Can you be such a person to someone, does this person even exist in your life, or is there any hope to develop such a friendship over time? How can we get through life without a friend? And when you are backed in a corner and it appears that no one is there, you are faced with the most difficult challenge, and everything seems hopeless, what will you do then? Give up, give in, or face it? The most important question is, will you do it all by yourself or will you face each moment that life gives you with someone who is willing to give it all for you? Are you willing to throw in the towel and give up on life without knowing you have a friend already there? This friend has already paid the price for you. He has given His life so you can have yours. He has loved you and will never leave you, even if you turn from Him. He will always be there right by your side, loving you until the very end. He doesn't care about what you do for him, because nothing you do could change what He already did for you. He sees beyond your inequities because He loves you. I have found this friend and every day I celebrate Him in my life. I believe in Him, His love, and what He has done for me. I stopped trying to prove myself worthy to Him, because I understand now that He loves me just for who I am. I don't have to pay for what He already did. He gave His life for me so I can have eternal life with Him. I don't become so discouraged any more as I live my life full of hope, faith, and love. I live to serve others because He served me. I live to give because what He has given me. I give because there is a new hope, a new inner peace, and a new light for my future. I know I have a friend and I walk with Him daily. I know without a doubt that He will always be there when I fall down, when I fail, and when I turn the wrong way. He will be there to pick me up, turn me around in the right direction, and be my light in any darkness. I have learned through all of life's challenges, through all of life's uncertainties, there is nothing more real than to have a relationship with Jesus Christ as your savior. He is what has brought me through the most difficult challenges, darkest days, and still stands strong through my daily walk. I

Friendship

walk with Him, knowing I have a friend who loves me unconditionally, and I love Him. He is the captain of my team who leads me personally, professionally, and in my family. He is a coach who wants everyone to be on a winning team. He is a strong leader who shows compassion, commitment, and love to all who follow Him. No matter what team you are on, no matter what you do, where you have been, He is the light of this world. He is the only one who will bring us out of darkness and show us the light. All we have to do is put our trust and faith in Him. Put all your other idols away and put Him first in your life and watch the transformation. Your life will never be the same. You will never feel separated, alone, afraid, or abandoned. People come and go, friends are not always reliable, trustworthy, or committed, but He is. He will never leave your side, He will always be there for you, guide you, and love you, even when you are most unlovable. He is God, the Father, the Son, and the Holy Spirit. Whoever believes in Him will have eternal life for He will be with you all the days of your life. Can you truly find a friend like this anywhere else? Are you willing to take time out of your life to get to know Him? I believe, with Him on your team, you cannot fail, lose, or do wrong. When God is in your life, it is so easy. Life is a lot like a game of baseball, you need a great coach. Who is better for the job? Who is willing to lead the team with courage, strength, and pure love? Are you willing to trust Him to be your coach? Through every season, I know that He will love me until the day I die. There is no greater friendship than the friend that

Losing is NOT an Option

I have found in Jesus. Through every game, you may win or lose, but with Jesus, you always end as a winner in the end. Trust me, I have been through many challenging games. I have made mistakes, experienced failures, and saw no hope. I have been in the valley of darkness, but the only light was knowing I had a God who was bigger than all my problems. He was the one who led me to a better place. A place where I have joy, comfort, and peace in my heart. I have turned my hopelessness and hurts, into praise and thanksgiving for what He has done for me. I have a new spirit, life, and future in knowing I have a Savior who loves me more than I love myself. I could not have done it all alone, for it was when I gave up all my pride and asked God to be my leader is when my life turned around. I found a new life, a new beginning, and a new hope for tomorrow. I still have faced many challenges, failures, and hurts in my life, but I did not do it alone. I had a friend, a true friend who was willing to walk beside me to show me the light. The game can bring us to our knees, crying for a way out, but He will lead you all the way home. He loves you and will protect you through every curve ball in the game. Some days, we are afraid and bail out as each pitch thrown at us is more than we can handle. We struggle in the game because we don't have the strength to go the distance, but He carries us through every game. When the lights go off in the stadium, I want to know I have a loving God waiting for me to come home, with loving arms saying, "Good game child." Except, after there is no more games to play, I will know true victory was won

Friendship

because I will be with Him forever. I have learned that the only way to "keep your head in the game," is to know that Christ is your Savior! Amen. God bless you and I hope you join God's team. Remember, with God as your coach, "Losing is Not an Option," because you're on a winning team!

It's not even the first inning and some people bail out

Galatians 6:9 "Let us not become weary in doing good, for at the proper time we will reap a harvest if we do not give up" NIV

Yes, life can send you a curve ball, but each player has to be ready to face the challenges that come with playing the game. Some take the game for granted and believe they are on top of the world because they are studs. They come with a false confidence that does not take into account that there will be struggles in the game. They underestimate the talents of the opposing team and only think of another easy win. They walk up to the plate with no plan of attack, arrogance, and a poor attitude, because they believe they are just that good. Except, it does not always follow the course they planned. Then, when the game takes a turn, they cannot handle the outcome so they bail out. Surprisingly, the game is only in the first inning with only a few runs behind, so they think it's all over. They lose heart, faith in overcoming a challenge, and discount what they are made of inside. They bail out, while forgetting what they trained for, so the team ends up losing a game that was meant to be won.

Life can be handled in the same fashion. People approach life with a defeatist attitude. They have no plan of action, strategy, or confidence that they can face a challenge and survive. They have an over inflated idea of what lies ahead, so their approach is total doubt that they can handle it. They surf through life with an idealistic view of dreams, ideals, and plans for the future. They act as if nothing matters and react with little interest in what lies in their path to stop them. They don't realize that life can throw you a curve ball, but they believe it will be all smooth sailing ahead. They become accustom to having things work out without too many struggles. The problem occurs when life does throw them a major curve ball, as it always does, so they bail out. They quit before they even start their journey and forget that some goals just take a little effort. They step out of the batter's box just to look at the coach with confusion, wondering why they struck out. This is just like the players who blame the umpire for a bad call and think life is just not fair. They become victims and do nothing about what happens in their life, just to sit on the side lines and watch life pass them by. Is life that unfair or difficult to handle when things go wrong? Is life merely a one-time chance to accomplish you're aspirations? Is it that difficult to plan for setbacks, obstacles, or failures with another approach? Do you just stand at the plate and watch three pitches go right by you and stomp back to the dugout blaming everything and everyone else for your failures? That seems the approach most juveniles have and learn real quick that it just does not work when they don't get their way. They learn from parents who love them, that they cannot always get what they want, when they want it, because they teach them it just will not work. So, they eventually learn new strategies, approaches, and attitudes to obtain the results they desire to achieve. Except, many adults just still do not get it. They think they can act as juveniles and continue to get their way, without any care or concern for others. They will do whatever it takes to get what they want, when they want it, and step over anyone in their way. This may work for some time, but not for long. Sooner or later they face life challenges and realize that they don't have what it takes to accomplish their goals. When things become a challenge, they give up, even before the first inning starts. These are the people who don't finish anything in life, because they have a defeatist attitude. They think that everything will come their way, easy, so all they have to do is stomp and storm to get their way as a child. They soon realize that life just does not work that way. Then when they see a challenge, they rationalize that it is just not worth fighting anymore and give up. You can never give up on yours dreams, goals, or aspirations. You have to develop a plan, approach, and a positive attitude to go forward. You also have to factor in the challenges that may occur with each step of the way. You may not know exactly what lies ahead, but you have to be patient, persistent, and plan new ways to accomplish your goals. You cannot assume nothing will be easy in life and live with a determination that will push you beyond your limitations. You cannot throw in the towel before the first inning and sit on the side lines but keep battling in the game until you see you are on your way from first base, all the way home. It is too easy to sit on the bench and watch the game, but it takes a strong person who is willing to play the game all the way until that final inning. Except, when you face each challenge with optimism, you develop confidence, courage, and the conviction to keep playing each game, and each season, until the very end.

It's NOT a ONE MAN Game

Galatians 3:9 " If anyone thinks they are something when they are not, they deceive themselves." NIV

Baseball is not a one man game, it's a team effort. You win as a team and lose as a team. It involves everyone participating in the final outcome, giving their absolute best effort they can offer. Everyone on the team comes to the table with different skills and plays various positions. The team achieves victory when they all work toward a common goal and focus on the team effort. Although, there are those players who think that it is all about them. They play the game as an individual, selfishly, and as if they are the only one capable of taking the team to the championship. Many people in life play exactly like these players and they end up with major disappointments and find themselves alone. They only consider their effort worthy of success and discount others in the process of improving their game. They stay focused only on their individual wants, needs, and desires. In doing so, they leave out the people who can offer them so much more value in their lives. They walk on by, as if they just don't matter or exist just to prove that they can do it without them. Victory is not won alone and it takes the people who love and support you the most to get you there. The celebration of victory should be with the team of dedicated individuals who rallied by your side, fought the fight, and loved you all the way until the end. Many teams fail because of selfish players who don't rely on or honor teammates in playing the game. The team loses heart and spirit as a result of such conduct and attitude. The winning team knows that they must depend on each other for their spirit and gifts to move forward. The winning team does not stay stagnate, but plows forward with the confidence, conviction, and courage to defeat every challenge and win every game as one. Remember it's the team, the team, the team that takes you to victory!

Rocked on the Mound

Timothy 1:7 "For God gave us a spirit not of fear but of power and love and self-control."NIV

There are going to be those days where you get rocked on the mound. You have to stay on the course, keep your eyes on the target, and never let your enemy know that they got the best of you. Life can be tough and it takes true character to get you through the difficult moments. The most difficult moments are what molds you and shapes you to be the person you were meant to be. It is in those times that the greatest life lessons are learned. You know it will not always be easy, but you have to hold your head up, command the mound, and look the batter straight in the eyes, to send a strong message that you are in control of the game. That is the problem in life, when people let others take control of their game, and allow other's behaviors affect the outcome. You have to know that facing those giants takes courage and staying true to who you are. Over time, you have been trained to be the best you can be, so allowing the game to get out of control will only cost you in the end. It is so important to take charge of your life and use your many gifts for creating positive outcomes. Everyone gets discouraged, but the best way to over come that is through determination. You have to turn discouraging thoughts, fears, and anxieties into the reality of who you are and meant to be. Your inner strength will guide you through the game, and your determination will produce positive results. Life lessons can only build you stronger inside, to be relentless, confident, and dedicated to your dreams. If you don't let the game take the best of you, those life lessons can only help you in the end. So, even if the game ends in a loss, you can walk off the mound with your head held up high knowing that you gave it your all. Everyone gets rocked in life, but not everyone gets defeated just to quit the game. Life will rock you time and time again, but when you face those challenges with the right approach and plan, you will see victory.

Step Up to the Plate

Corinthians 9:24 "Do you not know that in a race all the runners run, but only one receives the prize? So run that you may obtain it." NIV

I see a huge problem in the game when players don't "step up to the plate." They don't challenge themselves to be all they can be. Sometimes they become underachievers who don't give all that they have. Other times, they lack the drive, self-confidence, to see beyond their limited expectations. Players need to understand that it takes heart, passion, determination, drive, talent, and, most importantly, vision. They have to be able to see themselves for who they are and be willing to give what it takes to become the best they can be. They have to see results of their efforts and push themselves harder than they ever could imagine. Looking at where they want to be and being able to get there takes time, commitment, and perseverance. You have to have realistic goals, a time table, and a plan on how to get to your destination. This takes a person out of their comfort zone and into a whole new playing field in the game. You have to be able to visualize exactly what you want to accomplish. For some, they may feel that they want to take their talents to the next level, pursuing teams to assist them to open doors of opportunities. This is no easy task when challenging oneself to the next level. Others may feel the need to stay in the place where they started but desire to develop their maximum potential for the team. Whatever the goals are, it says a lot about the person who is willing to challenge themselves to meet them head on. It requires them to step up to the plate and discover the endless possibilities they have within them, to make their dreams come true. What they have to realize is that this doesn't happen overnight. This takes time, patience, commitment, and endurance. You cannot achieve your goals in a flash moment, like a lightning bolt coming out of the sky. It may takes weeks, months, or even years to get to your desired destination. The reality is that you have to have a time table of when you want to get there and put in the work along the way. In addition, you have to be confident that the work will pay off over a period of time and, if it's not, you have to go back to the drawing table to come up with a better plan. You have to evaluate each step of the way, to see if you're heading in the right direction without veering off course. Life sometimes takes you on a rollercoaster ride when we have goals to accomplish; it's never that simple or easy. Just when you think things are heading in the right direction, something gets in the way of what you want to achieve. You may come to a setback, such as an injury, which can surely set you back for a while. What you have to determine is your willingness to allow the setbacks to stop you from moving forward. It may take you off of your original time table, but you have to judge if it's worth it to continue the journey. You have to continue with your plan of action to get to your destination without giving in or giving up. Many players quit after failures or challenges along the way, but these are choices that they will have to live with the rest of their lives. Others still battle until the end and achieve their dreams and goals. They will always stand strong, knowing what they endured to achieve victory. This accomplishment gives them vindication of staying the course without bailing out. The proud moment of seeing your accomplishments gives you such relief, pride, and joy. This says so much about your character, because you were able to step up to the plate, not giving up, battling each obstacle, and moving on until you get to your desired goals.

    Life is just like this, with people who are trying to accomplish their many dreams and aspirations. They have to step up to the plate to get that desired job, home, or whatever they desire to achieve. Many people, like the baseball players, will give up when faced with challenges. They will stay in that job forever just because they're too afraid to step out of their comfort zone. They may also be afraid to challenge themselves to do more. Requiring more of themselves may make them feel awkward, ashamed, or belittled. They may not realize they do have what it takes to take it to the next level too. Maybe someone told them that they can't do it or they have it stuck in their head that they are not worthy of more. This negative talk can stick with a person for a lifetime. Instead, a person who has a vision, plans for the future, pushes themselves beyond their limited expectations, will see results. This doesn't happen overnight but requires a realistic plan, support from others, and effort. Nothing happens without a person putting their time, talents, and passion into something to make their dreams come true. They may experience hardships along the way, but they have to be willing to overcome each obstacle. This may also turn back the clock on when they were expecting to arrive at their goal. Allowing this to stop you will only deter you further from ever meeting your desired dreams. Sometimes life happens, people have financial, health issues, family issues, and life in general is again like a roller coaster. Just when you think you're about to get off the ride, it takes you for another spin. This is where you have to be willing to go the distance and stay the course. You may have to alter your plans, change your timeline, or dig in even harder. The most important thing is not to quit. You have to rise up and face your giants in life, challenge yourself to give more, and have the courage to continue on the journey. Eventually, you will reap what you sow and see the trophy. You may get that new job, degree, house, car, or whatever you were aspiring to do. This will give you great joy in seeing what you accomplished and satisfaction knowing what you endured to get it. This says so much about who you are inside and this will give you confidence to further your life goals and dreams. The most important lesson in baseball and life is that you have to step up to the plate. You have to be willing to push harder, longer, and not give up. The attitude going forward will always determine the outcome. Some people in life will bail out, step out of the batter's box just to sit on the bench. While others will step up to the plate and knock one out of the park. It's all up to you and how you want to approach the game of life!

Just Let it Go

Proverbs 29:11 "A fool gives full vent to his spirit, but a wise man quietly holds it back." NIV

Baseball can be an adventure of a life time with all the drama. The challenges within the game are enough to create havoc in any player's life. The team has to battle each and every game for a win. This comes with a price of putting your best efforts forward. Even with everyone contributing their absolute best, there will be those days that facing defeat is just part of the game. The emotional roller coaster can truly spin any person out of control, but with any ride that takes you in the wrong direction, you will just have to face facts. The times where the game becomes more than one can handle and emotions are at their peak, is the time, one must let it go. Players practice hard, are disciplined, and have tremendous passion for the game. They want to see those efforts pay off, in the game, for a win. Many players measure their success by how well they play and how many teams they beat. This can create a mix of emotions to always push yourself to a maximum level of accomplishment. The reality is that we are not always able to push our bodies to such extreme day in and day out. Our bodies do become fatigued, is at risk for injuries, and depends on our ability to meet its daily needs. We have to obtain plenty of nourishment, rest, and harmony. The problem lies in obtaining harmony and balance in a sport that demands excellence at all times. This results in players pushing themselves to their maximum potential and mental capacity before, during, and after the game. Sooner or later, mistakes happen and frustrations rise. The balance between the physical and emotional state of the game become disharmonious to oneself and this creates many problems. This creates many game changing moments as the players cannot produce the results that they desire. Then, the players push themselves even harder resulting in injuries, anger, hurt, and mental fatigue. During such times they become extremely distraught and cannot contain their emotions. This is the time to let it go, pick your-self up, and move on. For players should not measure themselves by how many times they fall down, but how many times they get back up and get back in the game. This requires self-control, a realistic perspective, and lots of support. All players will find themselves at their weakest moments but this is just part of the game. The one reassuring factor, is that many sports are not a one man show, but a team effort. You win as a team and you lose as a team. The game does not rely solely on one player to produce a win, it's a team effort. The most important part of the game is the ability to pick each other up when mistakes happen. Players must recognize when a team mate is in a slump and have the ability to encourage them to not be discouraged. The player who falters, also has the responsibility to not let it fester and let it go. This is not an easy skill to master with so much competition. Players have to create an environment of accountability, team work, motivation, and dedication. Of course this requires the proper leadership to gel the team together with a clear vision, team spirit, and a positive approach. Without proper leadership it can create an environment that fails to provide every player the opportunity to succeed. It's up to each player to hold themselves accountable for their presence on the team. Realistically, there will be times where leadership fails, players don't play as a team, and the environment is toxic. This is the time when you have to dig deep inside yourself, rise above the occasion, move on, and just let it go.

Life can be just as hard as a baseball game. It can be stressful, chaotic, and soon enough, spiral out of control. There will be times where we just cannot control everything in front of us. We can do our absolute best to come with a positive attitude, give our talents, role model exemplified behavior, and be part of a team. There will be those factors that we cannot change, because it requires accountability, truth, and leadership. People are not always accountable as they manipulate, lie, cheat, and steal their ways to the top. They will blame anyone and everyone in their way, to prevent their reputation from being tarnished. They are only worried about what happens to them along the way and will leave you high and dry after they get what they desire. There is no clear vision, no plan, and decisions are based on what is best according to their distorted vision. This type of leadership is poor and creates disharmony within any family, community, or organization. Eventually, people start becoming less worried about the team and more worried about saving their stance within the relationship. Many marriages fall apart for the same reason. Two people start off with the same vision, goals, and unity. The problems start when they become more concerned about themselves than the bond that started their relationship. Organizations can be compared to a marriage and, as it grows, the vision becomes unclear, goals are lost, and leadership fails to unify everyone. Instead, people take sides, become self-centered, and more concerned about their own agenda, forgetting the purpose of why they chose to join the company to begin with. Just like a baseball team who loses focus, people spiral out of control in pushing themselves to achieve their own desires. They too may work too many hours, burn the candle at both ends, and not nurture themselves in the process. This creates undo stress upon the family, job, and organization. Over time, mental fatigue, burn out, and mistakes start to become noticeable. The frustration rises within the person to a point that they start spinning out of control. This does not create a healthy environment, nor does it assist others within the process of building a solid foundation. Any relationship cannot stand such havoc, so it slowly grinds at the core, resulting in failure. This is the time to take responsibility to get the help required to get you back in the game. People try to put way too much on their plate and eventually things start falling apart. They do not have a realistic view of themselves and believe they have to do it all for the people who depend on them. This is as ludicrous as requiring a pitcher to pitch a perfect game each time he steps up to the mound. We are not perfect, we make mistakes, we have many weaknesses, we cannot put the whole world on our shoulders, and believe that everything is dependent upon us to handle. No team, marriage, organization, or any union that depends on only one person can survive this way. It's not a one person team; it is a team who comes together for the good of the team. Failures do happen, but we pick each other up, not compound it with personal attacks. A team with a leader provides a clear vision, works towards a unified goal, holds each other accountable, and creates an atmosphere of success. There will be times that this may be challenging, because we venture off course. The best thing to do when trials become too much to handle, your frustrations and self-doubt rise to a point that affects your personhood and those you most love, is just let it go. Let the frustration, anger, or anything that gets in the way of you moving forward, go. Take the time to collect yourself, refocus on where you are going, and start on a new path. Just don't let the game spiral out of control, take charge of your life, and just let the things that steal your joy go. Let it go before it takes you down a dangerous and destructive path to nowhere, zap who you are, and what you can do. Let it go by keeping your head in the game, move forward, and realizing your self-worth on the team!

Hitting a Wall

James 1: 2-4 "Consider it pure joy, my brothers and sisters, whenever you face trials of many kinds, because you know that the testing of your faith produces perseverance. Let perseverance finish its work so that you may be mature and complete, not lacking anything." NIV

Players will all eventually hit a wall. It may be an injury, loss of a game, or even personal. No matter how you look at it, it stops you in your tracts. Hitting a wall prevents you from moving forward to accomplish your goals. Many players become injured during the season and have to endure many months of rehabilitation even after surgery. They are taken out of the game they love and so desire to play. It seems like forever to conceive getting a chance to play again. The injury may be minor or may be a serious one. Sometimes, the injury may completely stop them from playing ever again. This can be devastating for the team, fans, and the player who has to sit out watching everyone else play a game which meant the world to them. During the season, each player gives so much to be a part of a winning team. The separation can be devastating and much anguish during the healing process. The disappointment, feelings of failures, anger, resentment, and frustration of not participating and giving your talents can come with a major price. This may cost the team big time, if the player was an asset to the winning season. More importantly, this may cost the player time, energy, and focus which sets him back from his goals. All the emotions that come with the letdown can be devastating as it builds up internally over the period of the injury. Many players cannot handle not being part of a team. They live for each moment of the game and look forward to the adrenaline rush from performing among so many fans. In addition, some players cannot handle losing a game because of pride, dedication, and the belief that they will not lose. Except, many players hit a wall, personally, during such tragedies and it becomes a part of their identities. The game is so vital that they cannot process doing anything more important and live for that moment when they are in the spotlight. So when personal hardships come their way and they are unable to perform at their max, they hit a wall. Some hit the wall harder than others, but sooner or later they all seem to hit it either head on or some seem to bounce off quickly. The latter is the best approach and is what separates the players who go the distance. What separates them is their mental approach. Playing the game comes with facing many obstacles, but how you face those obstacles is what prepares you for hardship. Having a realistic approach is a start. Going into the game with a poor attitude or an unrealistic approach only prevents you from moving forward. Thinking that you can do no wrong, are better than you are, you will never fail, or other realities of the game are just a matter of perspective. You have to realize that it's a game and there will be times you may win and times you lose. You may play your absolute best and there will be times where you play your worst. No player or team is guaranteed perfection at all times, it is not humanly possible. This doesn't mean you don't strive for perfection or your absolute best, but having a realistic approach knows better. You realize that life happens, injuries occur, better teams are out there, and personal issues may rock your best efforts. With knowing that you will face obstacles, assist you in preparing for them. The best coach prepares the team all season for areas that need to be improved upon. Coaches don't just go into the game with a winning season without a plan of approach. They study the other team, come up with plays, have back up players, and strategize new moves even during the game. This prevents the team from hitting a wall. Players need to have the same approach in their life and in the game. They have to prepare for rain and what they're going to do when the rain comes. They can hide out in the dugout or bring the umbrella full of ideas to play, even through the worst storm. There will be times when you slip in the puddles of hardship, get soaked with defeat, or even fall flat on your face from the winds that take you off your feet. Except, it doesn't mean you stand in the field waiting for the rain to stop, run for cover, or quit. It means you face each storm with a positive approach, attitude, and plan of attack? It means you work with the team of players and uplift each other instead of trying to do it on your own. You continue to battle through each storm, pick each other up, and continue on with a winning spirit. Hitting a wall doesn't mean you stop pushing yourself to a new level. It doesn't mean you throw in the towel, even when defeat happens. It means you realize that the wall is there as a wakeup call to help you change direction, focus, or how you're playing the game. Does it hurt, yes it does. The pain, hurt, frustration can be devastating, but quitting is not an option, it is a choice. You can sulk about it or get back in the game. This is the time to use the pain, hurt, and frustration to push yourself to a whole new level of playing, even if it takes you until the end of the season to get there. It's having the confidence, courage, and conviction to see what is before you. Maybe it's time to be real and see things you never realized to be true. Living in the truth is having the ability to face things with a clear vision and not lose heart of who you are meant to be. You are not meant to throw in the towel, but be the best person you can be to your team, family, but more importantly to yourself. Be the best person you can be so when you hit that wall, you will tear it down, walk over the blocks, and head in a new direction. Don't let the wall of disappointment, fear, rejection, or even failure stop you from being everything you are meant to be. Life is too short to allow any wall stop you if you allow it. Just like the game, we all face losses, injuries, and personal defeats. The most important lesson you can learn from the game is how to avoid hitting a wall and when you hit one, how to face it.

In life people hit a wall for many reasons: from financial failures, career, family, home, emotional issues, illnesses, diseases, and so many life travesties that can stop you in your tracts. People, like players, invest time, energy, resources, and so much of themselves toward the goals and aspirations they desire. Sometimes, they push themselves so hard they forget to care for themselves along the way. They end up with sickness, injuries, or emotional stress that can be a wall that halts them from moving forward. Some think they can do it alone and push others away, causing great pain and resentment of the people around them. When they realize they need their help, they pay the price of realizing the people they needed the most are not there for them. This wall can be emotionally damaging and can cause bitterness, anger, resentment, and so much grief. They dig themselves deeper in a hole by pushing people away and are not willing to admit their shortcomings. Instead, their pride gets in the way with recognizing their behavior and self-centeredness. They continue to hit wall after wall until they eventually self-destruct or come to terms that it's the very people who loved them, would have helped them through the hardship, if they only gave them half a chance to be in the storm along the way. Some people are wise enough to swallow their pride and reach out to others for help. They are the ones who rise above their circumstances, to a new beginning with a whole new attitude. Hitting a wall doesn't have to come with such a price, if you don't allow your pride and limited vision to halt new possibilities and solutions. People seem to wallow in misery for no valid reasons, only because they don't have a plan, vision, or are willing to change course. Just like a good coach, who has a game strategy, so do people have to have a plan for life. We will all hit a wall but, if we allow that wall to become a mountain of defeat then life has beat you. It is up to you to beat life by having a winning attitude, a plan of approach, and flexibility to make the necessary changes along the way. You cannot dig in so deep that you are unable to redirect, refocus, or change course. That is the perfect opportunity for failure to set in for sure. When you are willing to open yourself up to endless possibilities, relationships, and positive choices, your plan will be solid. You will continue to grow and develop the character, conviction, and courage to see your goals become a reality. You will move forward instead of allowing the wall to hold you back. You cannot continue to repeat the same mistakes again and again with the same plan or approach. It's when you can challenge yourself to become the best person in the game that you can be, you will be able to overcome tragedies. You will be confident to tear down the walls, climb over the bricks, but move forward to accomplish what you set your sight on. This may take time, may not work the first time, and you may have to come up with a new plan along the way, but failure is not an option. You can do it, it's not always going to be easy, but it is possible when you have the winning spirit. The only thing you have to remember is keep your head in the game!

When the Going Gets Tough, Get Going

Joshua 1:9 "Have I not commanded you? Be strong and courageous! Do not tremble or be dismayed, for the Lord your God is with you wherever you go." NIV

There is a saying about when the going gets tough the tough get going but seriously, it is just not that simple. Playing sports is very competitive and so is life. We come prepared to play hard, we come with the right attitude, equipment, and motivation that start the game or season off right. Although, in the midst of all the preparation, we forget the real reason why we came in the first place and get side tracked. We get so focused on the game, we forget about everything else going on around us. Focus is a necessity for playing sports, but reality always sets in. Reality reminds us of our limitations and prepares us to give more of ourselves. This can cause a great disappointment because we sometimes set our goals too high and forget that it takes time and endurance to get there. We live in the instant gratification world of today, everything about our lifestyle is fast pace. Well, we don't always achieve our dreams as easy in the world of instant gratification. We want everything now and become very discouraged as a result. This is when the going gets tough and the tough get going! The player must realize that his skills must be developed over time and becoming a competent, skilled player takes patience. The best approach is to dig down deep within yourself and go the distance. The player has to understand the limitations of his knowledge, skills, and aptitudes, but be willing to build on this daily. The player must be willing to be broken down, yet built back up learning new skills and approaches to the game. This takes strength of character, courage, and bravery. Eventually, the player will see great accomplishments both personally, professionally, and in the game. Quitting is not an option but when you push through hardship, great things eventually happen.

Life brings us the same lessons as in the game. We have many curve balls get thrown at us with different speeds, angels, and times. We have to be prepared to face each pitch with an attitude of determination, confidence, and motivation. There are times we will strike out and there will be times where we smack the ball to the other side of the field. This holds true in life, when we are in the midst of accomplishing our desired goals. There will be days when nothing seems to work for you and others where everything seems to plug along with ease. Nothing is impossible though when you don't bail out, look for new ways of attack, and be patient. Patience is so vital in life and yet the most important skill we overlook. We have to be willing to evaluate each step of our journey and determine if we are on the right path to meet our goals. We have to face each obstacle, with knowing that we can overcome them with a plan. Just like the batter finds new ways to attack the ball at the plate, so must we to pave our way to our desired destiny. The most important life lesson learned is we cannot do this on our own. Many try and fail, but it's the ones who are willing to put away their selfish pride, who will stay on the right path, and accomplish more than they believed possible. Asking for help is something that most players do. They have coaches who have played the game and know how to help them each step of the way, to be the best they can be. Tough people become even tougher when they have the guidance of others who support them to be their best. The help is not because they are weak and cannot handle the hurdles, but because it takes that special coach or friend to guide you. They can see things in you that you cannot, they can encourage you, when you are at your wits end, and they can love you even when you are not worthy of that love. A great coach or friend is what can make the difference between the tough get going and falling apart and bailing out of the game. We all struggle in life and we all have to face many difficult moments, but with people who love and support you can make all the difference in how you play the game. Some play the game and fail because of their stubbornness, selfishness, and poor attitudes. They are unwilling to change and continue to do it their way, only to find that their way sets them up for failure. Others, who are willing to do whatever it takes to be their best, succeed. They are open to learning, willing to change, and seek out people to help. Success doesn't happen overnight but, being willing to step up to the plate instead of sulking on the bench is the first step. Yes, the going does get tough, but to get going requires a plan, a positive attitude, discipline, hard work, dedication, and people who are willing to support you in making all your dreams come true. Get tough and get going, the people who love you the most will be at home plate waiting for you!

Accountability

Romans 14:12 "So then each one of us will give an account of himself to God." NIV

Accountability is a most difficult topic to discuss, because nobody wants to take any blame in the game. There is always someone to blame other than ourselves. We blame the coach for not teaching us the skills we need. We blame our teammates for failing to back us up in each play. They drop a ball, miss an easy tag, forget to call for the ball, and so many other mistakes that can create a losing spirit. Then when you cannot blame your team, you begin to blame the officials for poor calls. This leaves little room for self-reflection to how the individual player contributed or contaminated the game. A good player gets upset when performance is not to the desired level of play, but it is much easier to come up with excuses, rather than take responsibility for mistakes. Mistakes do happen to each and every player, but accountability is having the insight to own up to those mistakes and learn from them. Everyone is not perfect and everyone has strengths and weaknesses. When we gain confidence in our strengths, yet work on those weaknesses, is when accountability is achieved.

Accountability can strengthen not only yourself, but those around us. People do not look highly on arrogance and self-centeredness in an individual. Those kinds of people are so hard to be around, because they are always the center of the conversation and they have little desire to truly hear what you are saying. They almost believe that the world is centered on them and you are the only one there to meet their desires and expectations. They are poor team players, do not make a good friend, and are very difficult to live with. They may think that they are above the law or that they can manipulate others to obtain their desired outcomes without taking responsibility for their actions. This means they may lack the necessary changes to make positive outcomes for the future. Whereas some people have the ability to reach out to others, listen, be attentive, and even invest into making a positive impact on a negative situation. They seek to improve, uplift, and challenge themselves to a whole new level. They take responsibility, if things go wrong, by changing the course or finding alternative solutions for the good of all. Life requires us to move forward or it will leave you sitting on the side lines while everyone else is in the game. Many people chose to sit on the side lines because they do not want to take responsibility for anything. It is so much easier to

Accountability

watch everyone else do the work while they just enjoy the ride. They chose to live life for themselves and use others as a means to an end. They are egotistical, self-centered, and lonely people inside, because they don't understand how a special relationship with others can create a positive impact. People who are accountable seek and desire meaningful relationships. They are role models, team players, and a pleasure to be around. They understand that people are affected by their behaviors, attitudes, and temperament. They can self-reflect and make the necessary changes to make lasting impressions to the people around them. This kind of leadership is what moves teams to a championship level. Each team member is focused on making improvements to their individual play in an effort to improve the team as a whole. Team members become stronger and unite around a team spirit. This spirit is what moves them beyond their individual level of play but, to a higher level of oneness. The bonding that occurs as a result of this spirit uplifts each player to recognize that winning is not about one individual, but a group of individuals who are committed to each other and to winning the game. Accountability can move a team of individuals to not only win games, tournaments, championships, but to feel and believe in oneself as a victor. Achievement is more than winning a game, but being the best person one can be. Accountability is a reality check to facing failures, but also recognizes failure is not the end, but only the beginning to improving your game and being the best at it!

Fear

Joshua 1:9 New International Version (NIV)
"Have I not commanded you? Be strong and courageous. Do not be afraid; do not be discouraged, for the LORD your God will be with you wherever you go."

Fear enters the mind of a player and destroys their self-worth. Fear works on the mind but, over time it transitions to how you play. Fear is an evil that destroys the heart, soul, and mind of all those that it takes hold of. Players have so many fears that develop over time. The greatest fear is that of failure. No player wants to fail as they all dream of making great accomplishments and strive to be the best. The problem arises when fear takes over their spirit, so players begin to question their ability and this dampers their dreams of success. They wonder if they are good enough, may believe that others are better, and start feeling a lack of self-worth. Soon, fear will start to let this effect how they play the game. This can create havoc in the game and cause the team much harm. Eventually, the team becomes stifled and harmony is lost as a result. Everyone faces fears, but when fear becomes a dominant force in one's life, it can entangle deep inside, like a weed growing in a garden. The weed strangles all the plants and sucks all the nutrients meant for the plants. As a result, new plants cannot grow, and the remaining ones end up dying. Fear is only real in a person's mind and must be controlled and eliminated from taking root. Fear creates hopelessness when allowed to harbor into one's soul. This fear must be stopped early by developing a realistic or deeper meaning of life with a solid foundation. Facing the truth may be difficult at times, because people believe in their own version of truth according to their perceptions, values, and beliefs. Not everyone believes or defines truth the same way. People may distort the truth to protect themselves or others around them. They take the easy way out of difficult decisions, don't want to be held accountable, and ignore people who point out flaws in their character. The opposite of fear is truth, and without truth, life is nothing but a lie. Many people would rather live in a lie because it works for them. They don't have to face any changes or consequences of their actions. They may even believe that the lie will not hurt anyone, if they can convince themselves it is justifiable. They begin to cover things up, distort facts, and create more lies to cover up for previous ones. Fear of failure, rejection, and

Fear

all fear leads to avoidance of the truth in knowing and doing what is right. Fear can paralyze you when you allow it to fester. Some people have to seek professional counseling to discover ways to deal with individual fears. Others may face fears head on as a challenge to obtain personal, professional, and spiritual growth. They realize they have the skills to rid themselves of any fears they may face. Fear is a tangled weed and must be separated from a flourishing plant. People have to develop the life skills necessary to entangle the weeds in their lives. They have to separate the fears from reality and develop a strategy to handle problems that come their way. Fears will diminish when faced head on with a plan of attack. Over time, confidence is achieved, along with personal growth, and development. This builds on individual character to accomplish desired goals, gratification, and integrity. There is just no limit to what you can achieve when you become fearless.

Hurting the Team

Ephesians 4:32 New International Version (NIV) "Be kind and compassionate to one another, forgiving each other, just as in Christ God forgave you."

Many players become disgruntled throughout the season. They put a great effort into the game without realizing it's a team effort. Disappointments, failures, and trials are a major part of the game. Knowing how to deal with hurt is what will take each player beyond their limited expectation. They need to learn how to deal with so many hurts that come from poor outcomes. The most difficult hurt to deal with is when players hurt others on the team from their selfish attitude and behavior. Players can change this when they take ownership of their individual attitude, behavior, and actions. This is what separates a winning team from a losing one. It hurts to lose, but it will hurt even more when you lose the people around you, who do not contribute to a winning team. Team players can cause deep hurt, frustrations, and mistrust, but how you deal with this is what can be a game changer on the team. A team of players can contribute or contaminate the relationships. Contamination leads to hurt, inevitable losses, and failures. Each individual player can play for themselves to obtain their desired results. They may do whatever it takes to draw the attention to their stats, individual plays, and show boat their talents. This also creates deep rooted resentment among the other players who play for the benefit of the team. They give credit to other players for great plays, humble themselves in the media, and focus on contributing to a team winning effort. This behavior eventually creates a winning spirit in the team, uplifts players who are down, and gets more attention from the stands. People want to see a team who plays as a team, who believe in each other, who are dedicated to a team winning effort. It's not about one individual player, but a team of players who work together as one unit. They can accomplish even more than winning a game, but a brotherhood that takes them through the game of life.

    I'll tell you a story about how to deal with hurtful people. You cannot fixate on what they have done, cannot change their behavior, and you cannot control them. Unless a person takes responsibility or acknowledgment for their part in the relationship, own up to what they have done, and truly get how they have hurt others, they will never repair what was broken. Some people don't hurt others intentionally, but with little regard to how they treat others. They are so fixated on their own self that they don't see how their behaviors affects others. Many people go around life as if they have to be fed constantly. They are self-absorbed, needy, and believe the world exists to serve them. Unfortunately, few people are givers and so many are takers. Many people are clueless somedays, but they don't hurt others intentionally. Now, it is the INTENT that makes a difference in how we treat others. People have certain beliefs, values, and desires that motivate them to behave in a certain way. They act on those thoughts to obtain the results that they perceive as necessary at the time. Sometimes, they don't think about the long term consequences of their behaviors, but only focus on the here and now. This may cause some serious consequences to others around them. They may not even realize how this may contribute or contaminate relationships or circumstances around them. They just focus on what they want, when they want it, and the good feelings they achieve from obtaining the desired results. While others around them have to make compromises to assist them in their desires, this can cause some undo stress on the relationship over time. Eventually, the people who are affected by the selfishness become tired of being manipulated to meet the desired outcome, especially when they get nothing in return. This behavior continues as long as it is fed and the desired results are achieved. The behavior will diminish when others or circumstances around them can no longer be manipulated to continue the destructive behavior. They soon figure out they cannot continue to behave in that manner, so they either stop the behavior or move on to others who will feed their wants and desires. The manipulating behavior will leave a feeling as a victim or victor. When people obtain the results they desire through manipulation, they become the victor. Contrary, people feel as a victim when they don't get their way. They may even become belligerent to others, destructive, or further manipulate to obtain their desired results. A competent and mature individual will own his or her part in the relationship: take responsibility to repair the damage and change attitudes and behaviors that create positive changes for the future. When you think selfishly, you always hurt the people around you with or without realizing it. People who are team players think to benefit the people around them and the team. Life gives everyone a choice, to be a team player who contributes to a winning team, or to play for oneself. Just think of how much enjoyment in life one can obtain from being a team player. When the team wins from everyone contributing their absolute best, it just does not get any better. You're all winners in the end!

Bad Attitude

James 1: 2-4 "Consider it pure joy, my brothers and sisters, whenever you face trials of many kinds, because you know that the testing of your faith produces perseverance. Let perseverance finish its work so that you may be mature and complete, not lacking anything." NIV

Many players develop a bad attitude during the season. The tensions are high, the challenges can be overwhelming, and facing so many disappointments can create such an approach to the game. Players start the season off fresh and with a willingness to give the game their all. The game can have many bumpy roads that take the excitement away and turn it into turmoil. Sometimes players discover that they were fooled about promises made by managers, other teammates, and how it all turns out in the end. This creates frustrations, disappointment, and despair to overcome barriers that were not originally anticipated when the season started. Other times, players have too high expectations for desired outcomes and set their stakes too high. Often, failures follow the unrealistic goals set and become even more challenging to pick oneself up from the blow. The game can result in many disappointments during the season, for many reasons. Players must face these challenges, make necessary changes to their attitudes, and not allow the frustrations to get in the way of their game. Not always so easy, when you're dealing with personal relationship issues. Relationship issues can be a game changer.

The greatest relationship disappointment comes from issues with trust, commitments, and expectations of others. Life can send us many trials and errors of failed relationships that end for no valid reasons. People do come with personal flaws, that disappoint others, when they are not honest, reliable, or trustworthy. Personal character is important to develop in life so that others can respect you. Becoming a person with character is not always easy but, putting your best effort forward can improve so many relationships developed along the way. Lying, cheating, and hiding behind problems is no way to prove oneself to others. People despise others who use others for their own personal gain or satisfaction. People do depend on others for their time, friendship, and help in accomplishing goals, but not at the expense of the relationship. Taking others for granted is a serious offense and should be always considered

Bad Attitude

when depending on others for help. People do care to help but, it gets tiring when it's all about them. A relationship should be give and take, not just take and take. A person will become hurt, frustrated, and develop a bad attitude as a result. This creates a feeling of being used and abused with no appreciation in return. A selfish relationship is cruel to develop and always leaves long lasting scars as a result. No matter how many favors one asks of others, giving back praises or some kind of appreciation is always best. In life, we need each other to help during difficult times. We need friends, team players, and family who are willing to be there to pick us up when we fall down. Although, recognizing when those favors are crushing the other's willing spirit should be always a top priority. People need to show love back to others and strengthen the relationship with kindness, appreciation, and loyalty. A bad attitude can develop from many disappointments but, can be changed with showing love in return. Never take people for granted, show others you care, and lift up each other along the way. People who just use others for their personal gain show absolutely no remorse and can destroy others in the process. Develop character to demonstrate compassion, commitment, and love to that special person who gave you their all!

Underachievement

2 Timothy 4:7 "I have fought the good fight, I have finished the race, I have kept the faith." NIV

Players must determine exactly how much they are willing to put into the game. They have to be willing to go the distance, even when pressures, injuries, or other obstacles deter them from obtaining their goals. There are going to be times when the pitcher gets rocked on the mound, batters are unable to hit any curve ball, an outfielder drops a simple fly ball, and the momentum of the team starts to become rattled as a result. Players become disgruntled and start calling each other out, coaches temper start to fly off the handle, and the fans become majorly disappointed. Ok, now what? What exactly is each player going to do at this key point in the game? Does the team just pack up and go home, do they just go through the motions and complete the game, or do they become angry at their team for making so many mistakes? Is this what the game is all about or is there more? At this point, each player has to own up to his responsibility and make some necessary changes. Players have to honestly evaluate their actions, behavior, and attitude toward the poor outcomes. The most important aspect of any team is the realization that everyone is not giving their absolute best. Underachievement can be a game changer in sports and in life. Athletes are always under the gun to give more, worker harder, and perform at their best. Anything less can result in poor plays that eventually lead to a major loss. Underachievement is determined when players gives less than their absolute best to the team. They don't come prepared to play the game as they were trained. They are not focused, they are physically exhausted, they show up to play, but their actions are just not producing desirable results. They eventually wilt under pressure and the team suffers as a result. The coach has more choice words to say to his team during such times, but change must come from within. Each player has to develop the character, courage, and confidence to hold themselves accountable for their actions, dig deep within to push a little harder, and remember why they were called to be a part of a team.

    Sports and life can be a challenge, push anyone to their limit, and at times, you just fall apart. Challenges can create uncertainties within an individual that start a process of self-doubt, lack of effort, and failure to live up to your potential.

Underachievement

This attacks the heart and soul of who you are, why you are here, and your purpose here on earth. A wall is built up that appears to be too wide and tall to overcome, so you cower. You start believing the unthinkable and it tears a piece of you down with each negative thought. You forget how hard you worked, and you just cannot see yourself getting to the other side. Really? Is this really what you're all about, are you going to high tail back and retreat, and are you going to give up even before you gave it a chance? How many times do people get to a moment in time where they just cannot face one more obstacle and they become stuck exactly where life leads them in time? But remember, this is a choice each player and individual has to make during every step of the game and in life. Are you willing to be a warrior or do you stay as a victim cowering to what life brings? People have choices to make when faced with challenges; there is no way out of it. Challenges have to be met with a plan of attack, a positive attitude, and a winning spirit. No challenge is too big to handle when faced with the right approach. Except, many people try to do it alone and fail. They try to be the hero or the lone survivor when it would be so much easier to ask for help. People try to carry the world on their shoulders and eventually collapse from all the weight. They push themselves too hard and fast without stopping for a break along the way. They become impatient, intolerant, and frustrated when they do not produce the desired results. Eventually, they change course, stop trying, and give up. They just don't want to do what it takes to accomplish their goals, so they underachieve. Underachievement is a way people take to sit on the bench in life while they watch others in the game. They give less of themselves, because they don't have a clue just how to face a difficult moment. They wonder aimlessly without any consequences to how their attitude and behavior affects others. They become angry at themselves, others, and have a difficult time owning their part in what happens as a result. Underachievement is a selfish trait that tells others your willingness to give is less than expected. At some point, you determine it is ok to check out of the game, do what you deem is necessary, and just go through the motions. This is juvenile behavior and should not be tolerated by a coach, employer, spouse, or anyone who depends on you. Taking responsibility for your actions is part of life, you have to be willing to give, not just take. This is a person who thinks the world exists to serve their every need and is unwilling to give of themselves for the betterment of others. There comes a point in time where you have to step outside of yourself, step up to the plate, and do what it takes to get the job done. People are always willing to assist you when you struggle, so asking for help is only natural. Sometimes life can be overwhelming, so enlisting key people to get you through those difficult moments would only benefit you in the end. The person who underachieves must decide to make a strategy in life to achieve. Each individual has to search for new ways, opportunities, and vision the end result. With a vision, a person can accomplish goals and achieve the unthinkable. This does require effort, determination, and failure cannot

Underachievement

be an option. Dreams are accomplished with a winning spirit and underachievement is nothing less than failure at its best! Each player on the team has to step up to the plate, give the team their absolute best, and never stop believing in each other. Life and sports are tough, but you have to be even tougher. That is how the game is won!

Dealing with Difficult People

John 15:12 "My command is this: Love each other as I have loved you." NIV

Dealing with difficult people is part of the game. Coaches have to deal with players, parents, umpires, and even the fans. The coach has a most difficult job keeping everything in control, even when it is not. Players lose their tempers, parents become disgruntled, umpires can make or break a game with a bad call, and fans can be loud and obnoxious. In all this chaos, the game must continue and the coach has to stay focused. Decisions have to be made and not everyone will agree with them. Players get upset because they may have to sit out an inning or not play in their desired spot. Parents may become impatient when they see their child is not in the game. Umpires become disgruntled when coaches challenge their calls. Fans don't always stay quiet in the stands, and may shout out inappropriate comments to add even further tension to the game. In all of this drama, one team wins and loses. Players have to give their best even when everything is falling apart, but they sure have to depend of each other for a winning season.

Life is so much like the game of baseball, we deal with difficult people all the time. We depend on them at home, at work, and in our social experiences. The problem is trying to get along without so much conflict and drama. People can either contribute to your success or contaminate it, just like in the game of baseball. There are people who value others around them and lose touch with what they may get from the relationship. People are not always conscious of their selfishness, but it sure does damage the relationship when they continue to focus on only their desires. While others are team players who focus on the best for all involved, many can damage the team by focusing on what is best for themselves. We don't live in a perfect world and we have to learn to master the art of human relationships. The key is to not let others deter you from being the best you can be. You cannot change others, but you can change your attitude, behavior, and choices to create the desired outcomes you want. Unfortunately, there will be times where the consequences of someone else's decisions will create undesired outcomes in your life. Parents, children, employers, and many people in your life will dictate decisions that have an effect on outcomes. This leaves you with little choice but to clean it up or move on. Except, when you personally make choices that damage relationships, create chaos, or cause poor outcomes, there is nobody to blame except yourself. People have to make decisions based on outcomes that keep in mind others around them. Decisions have to be made with a win-win attitude, not with an I win you lose ideal. In baseball, a coach keeps in mind everyone to create a win-win solution. It is not always easy but planning is key in our decision making process. We must use our critical thinking skills, developed over time to understand what will work and what will not. We have to evaluate the pros and cons of our decisions, without making rash decision that will eventually come back to haunt us. The most important input in our decisions is how they will affect the people around us. People in our lives can be difficult and put a damper, even on the best planned events, but one must keep in mind that there will be set backs. Goals become stifled when a boss does not value an employee working diligently to move forward. People are difficult when they forget to value a team spirit. For it is the team that wins as a team, not as a selfish player. It is the team that can make victory happen. It is the team that can rise up and shine to show strength, courage, and dedication. It is the team that will take on challenges, overcome every obstacle, and fight to the end. The people who have that team spirit will be the ones to make their dreams come true. For it is with the right attitude, values, and behaviors in how we treat each other is what separates us from being difficult, to being determined to be the best we can be. There are always difficult people out there, but with a plan, purpose, and patience, anyone can overcome them with a winning spirit. Just focus on being a team player, develop a plan, move forward with it, and watch your dreams turn into a reality. Dealing with difficult people is part of the game, don't lose focus, the trophy is waiting in the end!

Taking Your Share of Lumps

2 Corinthians 12:9 "My grace is sufficient for you, for my power is made perfect in weakness" NIV

Every player will have to take their share of lumps. The game does not always go the way it should. There are going to be challenges, obstacles, victories, and defeats. Except the hardest ones to face is when it becomes personal. Players may be passed up by others who may have the edge over them or does not fit into the mold of what the coach desires. This is a hard lump to swallow to think that you are not good enough to play on a team. The player may ponder on his progress throughout the years and even question if this was all worth it in the end. Discouragement comes with a price that can make or break you in determining what destination lies ahead. Do you just quit or do you dig down deep within yourself to do what it takes to make it to that next level?

Life can throw you many curve balls: a loss of relationship, a job, or other setbacks that shake your confidence. The question always remains, exactly what are you going to do about it now? Do you pack your bags, have a pity party, and give up your dreams? That may be your first reaction, when faced with a personal defeat or setback, but will that accomplish your desired goals? Do you blame everyone and wait for opportunity to knock on your door or do you face failures with a new attitude? It is so easy to give up and sit on the side lines of life watching everyone else give of themselves? It is so easy to be the victim, finding all the reasons why you didn't get what you desired? You just cannot face the truth, life is not easy and it takes courage, commitment, and character to succeed. What will hinder you the most is a poor attitude. The attitude you take towards trials and tribulations will set a straight line to exactly where it will take you, nowhere. So, continue to pout, continue to blame, and continue to have all the excuses to prove to yourself that you cannot move forward to accomplish your dreams. That is what separates the winners from the losers in any game. Winners face challenges and obstacles, finding ways around them, not giving up until they obtain their desired goals. Losers sit back and blame everyone else why they did not make it. Yes, life is hard and we face many challenges that may set us back for months or even years, but are you worthy of obtaining your dreams? Are you willing to do what it takes to find new ways, change behaviors and attitudes, and work harder than you have ever done before? This is what each player has to determine to be the best at what they do. Each player has individual talents, knowledge, skills, and opportunities to succeed. The issue is not if they are good enough, but are they strong enough to not let roadblocks stop them from moving forward. The confidence from finding ways around those obstacles will only strengthen character and provide you a new inner peace to do it again, with new challenges that arrive. Nobody is exempt from problems, it is just a part of life. The game is a constant battle in a competitive playing field. The only way to victory is to realize that you can never give up hope! Play hard, be strong, stay focused, and never let your eye off the prize. Though you may fail time and time again, stay the course and remember it will all be worth it in the end. Who knows, maybe you will do even more than you ever imagined. A winning team is willing to go the distance!

Out of Control

Romans 12:21 NIV "Do not be overcome by evil, but overcome evil with good."

Baseball is an awesome sport to be a part of as a parent. You sit in the stands as you watch your kid play with such excitement. You observe how the kids work together to make that play happen. Of course you want the team to win, but at what cost? The game gets intense as both teams compete each inning to get a player to cross home plate. Except, with each play comes tremendous pressure for the kids to perform and produce. Players give so much of themselves to compete at this level. They invest endless hours of practice on and off the field. They may even hire personal trainers to assist them to perform at their max. They don't come to the game to lose, but one team eventually does in the end. With all of this intensity before, during, and after the game, comes great conflict within the game. Each team tries to win with a strategy to produce more runs. During this time, emotions rise as coaches become irate at umpires for bad calls, at players for mistakes, and at the parents who show disrespect. The players also become upset when their team doesn't produce the outcomes that they worked so hard for. They start blaming each other, get upset about calls, and feel the pressure from the disappointed fans. The parents can't help themselves at this point by yelling and screaming at the coaches, players, and umpires. They act as if nobody but them knows how to play the game. Fathers sit in huddles talking over the bad decisions the coaches made, make obscene jesters towards the umpires, and even start coaching their kids from the stands. This whole scene is out of control and can affect the outcome of the game. Sometimes, it gets so intense that fights break out, coaches get ejected from the game, and parents project verbal abuse towards the other team. Is this all worth it? Is this what you prepared your kid to endure? Do you think there is way too much emphasis on the winning and not on the quality of play during the game? Is a trophy worth cheating, lying, stealing, and fighting for? Where is the integrity and honor in the game when it gets so out of control? What lessons are you teaching your children when this happens? Does this prepare them how to face future challenges in their lives? How are we going to live in this world if this is how people behave to get what they want? Baseball is an excellent sport that teaches us so much about life, but how we play the game is exactly how we will deal with most issues in our lives. We either play the game with honor and integrity, or we play with deviant behavior to win at any cost. Many will quit because it gets too tough to handle. The game does become intense, but each player has to choose to either rise to the occasion or succumb to the challenges they will face. The best players understand the challenges within the game, are willing to face them, and find ways to overcome each obstacle in order to achieve victory.

Life can become out of control just as the baseball game does. People lose perspective of their lives and become emotional, illogical, and volatile. Life can start slowly, just as a baseball game with things running smoothly and not too much happening. Soon as obstacles occur, life becomes intense with having to face many decisions. People start to panic, they become uncomfortable with knowing what to do, and end up making poor choices. Just like the baseball game, as the game intensity gets heated up, so life can become stressful when situations happen that are not foreseen. This may happen in a marriage, job, or in life in general. People face many challenges relating from financial, health, spiritual, and relationship issues. These issues can change the game plan, put pressure on a person to make undesirable changes, or create disharmony within a life that was great. Tensions rise, emotions run ramped, and people spiral out of control. They lose focus and eventually create havoc in their lives and drag others in the mess. How does life get so out of control? Just like the baseball game, it seems to just ramp up over time and become a toxic environment to be a part of. Do we own the results with the decisions we make or are we victims who have no control in the problems? Do we just sit back and take it or do we take charge and find a plan of attack. When the game becomes intense and a team starts to lose, coaches have to derive new strategies to attack. They don't just throw in the towel and give up the fight. They take the fight to the team and battle back for a win. Remember the game is not over until the umpire says it's over. Life may be turbulent and give us trials, but we cannot give up the fight until our body is cold in the grave. Life is a game that has many innings to battle, as we fight to achieve our goals. We cannot give up and call it quits in the middle of the game. You have to keep your head in the game, command the mound, face the next batter, and deliver your best pitch. Once that ball is out of your hand, you cannot do anything about it until you try again to deliver your best pitch. Just like life, you cannot take back any mistakes, but you can change your attitude, behaviors, and choices to produce better outcomes. Some people go through life with no plan of attack, no moral compass, or have a clue what direction they are headed. When life throws them a curveball, they fall apart, loose control, and become victims to their poor choices. How many people make choices that cause them or someone else in their lives great harm? They act as if their behavior and choices have no effect on what happens in their lives, so they continue down the same path until they hit a brick wall. Then life is out of control and they don't know how to get back into the game. The decisions they make are made with little planning or thought process. This leads them down a dangerous and destructive path of no return. Just like a baseball game, you have to understand what you're doing, how you're doing it, and how you're going to get the results you want. This takes some critical thinking skills that many people do not use. They run their life on an emotional roller coaster, dodging and diving problems as they present. Life always brings us problems that can be so overwhelming that we need to consult assistance of faith, family, or friends to guide you through your decision making process. At times you are so out of your league that turning to professional help may be the best choice to lead you out of your circumstances. Some people believe that they can handle issues all by themselves and end up deeper in problems than they thought was possible. Life requires a vision to see the direction or place you wish to achieve. People cannot expect to accomplish their goals in a vacuum and land in the place they want to be. No, it just doesn't happen that way and that kind of thinking is dangerous. What people need is a game plan that knows who the players are, what the goal is, and a plan to accomplish it. People also need to incorporate flexibility and have the resilience to change direction or course. You cannot be rigid or stick your head in the sand waiting for things to happen for you. You have to take charge of your life by planning and paving the way to your dreams. You need to surround yourself with good people who will support you and uplift you along your journey. Most importantly, you cannot be a quitter. You cannot quit when things get rough. That is the time when you need to develop a will and determination to see it through to the end. Many ball games were not won in the first few innings. The game was won after battling through many difficult innings, not giving up the fight until the very end. Many games were won after the last play because the players dug deep inside, stuck together, and delivered results. Life should be looked at the same way; you cannot expect results to happen overnight. It takes courage, confidence, and conviction to stay the course and see it all the way to the end. You have to understand what it will take to achieve your dreams, but you have to have the right attitude to see those dreams come true. You cannot do this with guilt, anger, or shame, but with a positive approach and attitude. Life can become out of control, but with a moral compass, you can surpass obstacles, develop the right attitude, and lead in a positive direction.

I base my moral compass on the foundation of Jesus Christ. He leads me with the right attitude, approach, and in the right direction. His word as written in the Bible is what I lean on to maintain my focus. I cannot do things by myself, but with Jesus Christ by my side, I can do so much more than ever expected. There are times where I fall short of what He asks of me, yet by His Grace, I am forgiven, and I continue my journey with Him by my side. I believe in Him because what He has done for me. He paid the price by dying on the cross. Who would love you so much? Your life may spiral out of control but with Christ, He puts it back on the Road to recovery. I walk with Him each day and allow Him to lead me in the right direction. I have a plan that can be no greater than to serve Him in all that I do. This plan leads me down a road to success. Life can become out of control, but with the right coach leading the game, you can win. I just realized that I have the best coach in the whole world, Jesus Christ. I know I am on a winning team and victory will be mine, in the end, because I will be with him now and for all eternity.

Cancer Destroys a Team

Luke 6:27-28 NIV "Love your enemies, do good to those who hate you, bless those who curse you, pray for those who mistreat you."

Yes, cancer is contagious, contaminates, and destroys everything around it that it comes close to. Cancer is an abnormal growth that proliferates throughout the body but affects the mind, spirit, and will to fight. Just like cancer in the body, cancer can also affect a team and destroy it. It starts off small and can grow like cancer with each organization, player, coach, umpire, and fan. This cancer can be as simple as a bad attitude, selfish player, power hungry coach, ego driven umpire, an organization looking for prestige, or even a parent with unrealistic ideals. The problem that these issues cause is that it affects the cohesiveness of the team. This cancer spreads throughout the team and doesn't foster any positive growth and development. The team becomes stifled, as these issues are ignored and fester frustration, hatred, and disappointment among themselves. Players feed off each other when one player shows up with a bad attitude, it becomes a team problem. Many players show up thinking the game is all about them. They don't care about supporting their teammates, or not even willing to follow the coach's direction. They think they will do it the way they think is best. They sit in the dugout and complain about the other players' mistakes and criticize them relentlessly. Of course, they believe that they can do no wrong and forget that half the enjoyment of being a part of the team is being a team player. The power hungry coach can also be a nuisance for the team. This coach is unapproachable, big headed, rude, obnoxious, and is only concerned with his winning record. He doesn't try to develop players, he is only fixated on the trophy. This cancer spreads vehemently throughout the team and causes much distress. As a result, many parents will pull their kids off the team and many kids will just leave on their own. A coach's job is to build a team, not for his own glory, but the glory of all involved. Just like a coach, an umpire can create havoc too. Some umpires are not approachable and can be pretty obnoxious when making calls. Then you see others, who will joke around with the coaches, players, and even parents. This just makes the game so much more enjoyable than some tyrant who makes the games uptight and miserable. The fans can also make the game unbearable when they become out of control yelling obscenities throughout the game.

Cancer Destroys A Team

Of course they have unrealistic expectations of their kid, other players, umpires, and the coach. They act as if they can do a better job, but don't get involved or have civil conversations with the coach when problems arise. No, they yell at the coach in the middle of a heated game, threatening them to take their kid home and off the team, really? They also refuse to pay the dues on time or not at all, as if the team owes them for their kid's talents, really? This cancer creates tensions with other coaches, players, and even parents, because they feel threatened by their approach. Most parents are positive and cheer on all the kids, assist the team, and understand it's only a game. The organization suffers tremendous issues from these problems. Many baseball organizations fail and lose many good players. A good organization is comprised of a foundation of unity, character, positive environment, the ability to grow and develop, and enjoy the fellowship and each game. The organization is like the human body and needs all the parts to work together to create harmony. Just like cancer that gets in the body to disrupt the smooth operation, so it can destroy an organization if allowed to fester. Cancer can be a dangerous and destructive disease but can be treated with some harsh medications. The team also can be saved with some harsh realities, rules, and leadership. A team needs to come to the reality that winning will come as a team. Rules have to be in place to weed out attitudes and behaviors that cause disharmony within the team. A positive and proactive leader must be in place to develop and direct the team. There has to be a clear vision of what it will take to obtain success. Any cancer in the team must be eliminated before it starts growing. With a positive, not punitive leadership style, can set in place an environment that is cancer free.

Cancer is a dreaded disease and is a part of many families. Families not only have cancer that affects their body, but a cancer can also tear apart every part of the family life. Again, cancer starts off as a small abnormal cell that grows throughout the body if not detected early and obtain treatment. Cancer can start the same way in the family, just like on a baseball team. It can be with a poor attitude, parents who cannot agree, kids out of control, or even finances in disrepair. How does a family get so off course? It is just like when a disease is not detected and goes untreated. There can be complete denial on everyone's part, within the family. The dysfunction becomes part of their daily life. They argue, don't see eye to eye, are selfish, disrespectful, and can be violent. This eventually leads to dangerous and destructive behaviors that create chaos within the family unit. The family may be arguing about one thing, but don't see that there are deeper issues like control, selfishness, and unresolved anger that contributes to the problem. They get fixated on the trivial things that account for day to day stresses but don't take a step back to look at the bigger picture of what is really going on. Most families are so busy today with working, community involvement, and personal responsibilities that create tensions, that cause disharmony. Sometimes, it just takes someone to be the logical one and see what factors are creating such tensions in the home. It takes open and honest communication to admit the issues, without feeling the personal attack. Just like a baseball team, problems are not about the person; it is about the team or family. Facing problems has to start with a team approach. Everyone on the team has a role, responsibility, and contribution to make the team successful. When one team member goes astray, the whole team is affected by the person. The best approach is to not attack, but find a strategy that will allow for compromise, compassion, and creativity. This is the time to create a vision, find solutions, and develop a plan for success. The family cannot allow for cancer to cause division and distress, but it can be brought under control with peace, joy, and love. A family unit can be harmonious with proper leadership and everyone contributing, not contaminating the team spirit. They may need professional help doing this. Just like a baseball team, the family unit can enjoy each day, season, and year with unity, joy, and grow even stronger, so the next generation will follow in their footsteps.

I understand much about cancer and as a registered nurse and a person who was diagnosed with colon cancer over three years ago. I was always healthy, exercised, had a well-balanced diet, working two jobs, assisted in Sunday school, medical assistant for our football team, helped out in the school, a wife, and a mother of three boys. Our lives changed dramatically, as I had to quit both jobs as a Clinical Nurse Educator and RN who worked in the Investigative Care Unit. This cancer affected our finances, relationships, and the harmony within our home. We all had to make big adjustments in all areas. My boys had to learn to sacrifice financially, had to take on more responsibilities and become my warriors. My husband also had to develop the strength and character to lead our children in a positive direction. We did not want the cancer to affect the cohesiveness of our family, too. We decided to take a team approach with God as our leader. We turned to God for everything, we also had the support of our church, family, and our great community. The hardest part was telling my three boys about the diagnoses. The two high school boys took it in quite well, but my sixth grader truly didn't understand what the depth of this disease meant. We all sat around the living room in deep prayer and asked God to lead us the way. This was not going to be easy on anyone, but they tried to stay positive. If it were not for our relationship with God, we would have fallen apart. Cancer affects everyone involved and can shake up things everywhere. I was not going to allow the people around me to suffer needlessly by my attitude. I gave up control and decided to let God guide me every step of the way. I read scripture verses, prayed, and put all my trust in the Lord. I decided that I would give it all to God and I would be a witness to others with my strength. I did not want to be a victim, but a victor. I did not want pity, but prayers. I was going to handle everything with a team approach, with God as my coach. I did not focus on the bad things that can happen, but what good I can give of myself during this uncertain period of my life. I knew it was not going to be easy, but when you start off with the right approach, an

Cancer Destroys A Team

awesome coach, and a terrific team, I knew I could get through this. I just took each day as it came and still tried to be the best wife, mother, and friend I could be. I did not want the cancer to define me, but me defined by my walk with the Lord. I don't see myself as some religious fanatic, but a person who is far from perfect, and needs a Savior. I just decided that I could not do this alone, and realized this early on in my life. When I tried to do things my way, I failed, but when I walked with the Lord my life turned around drastically. This was how I met my fabulous husband. I asked God to find me a man who has the heart for the Lord and would be a great leader in our family. He has been a pillar of strength in leading our family. We are nowhere near perfect, but we rely on Grace each and every day. God is the one who we rely on for everything and we look to Him to guide us through all of our issues. I was going to allow God to strengthen our family during this ordeal. Within the first two weeks of my diagnosis I saw the oncologist, surgical oncologist, had a CT Scan, PET Scan, liver biopsy, tons of laboratory tests, and mediport put in. I believe I was so stressed out that it affected my stomach and I ended up in the Emergency Room one night at two a.m. for some fluids, X-rays, and medicine for my stomach. By seven a.m. I had to get to another hospital to have my mediport put in, that morning in the operating room. The following Tuesday, I started an aggressive chemotherapy regimen treatment. The hardest part was giving up so much what I loved to do. I have worked in the hospital setting for over thirty years. I spent thirteen years to obtain my BSN and, many years later, obtained my MSN in Nursing Education. I was so Blessed to have many students come and visit me, pray for me, and follow me on Facebook. I am also Blessed to have awesome co-workers, who have sent me so many gifts, prayers, and also follow me on Facebook for support. The people in my church have uplifted me, especially my women friends in my Bible study. My family has helped me within the house but also keeps my spirits up. My sixth grader made me a poetry book as part of his assignment in class, dedicated it especially to me. He gave it to me for Christmas and I wept tears of joy that my kid could say such beautiful things from his heart. I see the hand of God working in my family, with their love and support. I am so proud of them, that worlds just cannot explain. I have endured a colon resection after ten rounds of chemotherapy, liver wedge resection after eight more rounds of chemotherapy, two rounds of radiation therapy, and still continuing chemotherapy until today, over three years later. Cancer may be in my body, but not allowing it to divide our family is what is most important to me. Just like the baseball team, life throws you so many curveballs. This one went directly over the plate and blew past me. Except, with each passing ball I was ready this time. I knew that I was not going to let the next one by without a fight. I knew that I could conquer anything in the game because I have a coach who loves me and will lead me all the way home. God gives me joy, hope, and love, all I have to do is "keep my head in the game!"

Losing the Big Game

1 Peter 5:7 NIV "Cast all your anxiety on him because he cares for you."

Now, every player will face some challenges and losing the big game is all part of the process. Defeat is no easy feeling and you have to be able to suck it up, just like the best of them. You play the game hard, do all the right things, and at the end, the score just does not add up in your favor. Defeat can knock you off your feet, crush your spirit, and make you want to quit the game. Yes, many players quit the game during such difficult times and walk off the field, as if the game never even mattered at all. Others will get back in the game to try again, develop a new strategy, and improve their skills. They figure out what works best and play even harder, at the game they love best.

Losing is NOT an Option

Life can send people many losses, but learning how to recover is what separates those who achieve their dreams from those who don't. Developing a new attitude, skill, and with determination, those dreams can turn into reality. It takes courage, conviction, and confidence to pursue positive outcomes. People sometimes just don't have the patience to wait very long, or the desire to overcome the obstacles along the way. They check out of life and watch on the side lines while everyone else is playing the game hard. They turn to alcohol, drugs, or other addictions that destroy their lives permanently. Then, when it is too late to re-enter the game, they quit altogether, suffering tremendous physical and emotional consequences. While others gut it out, suck it up, and do what it takes to finish each inning with success. With each inning they face, they become even more convicted to face the next one with their head help up and eyes fixated on the prize. Winning the trophy is the ultimate victory, but not every game ends with a win. The life lesson comes with what we do and how we face those tough losses. The attitude we take toward those losses will determine if we can move on in the series toward the final game. Moving beyond the losses and into the next series is what winners do. The game is not over yet, so pick up the bat and hit the field. One big loss does not mean it is all over. The game has to go on and you just find a new approach to the plate!

Knowing when you're on a losing team

Exodus 14:14 NLT "The Lord himself will fight for you. Just stay calm."

You have to know when you're on a losing team. Many players stomp their bats and pout in the dugout when they realize that they are losing. I've seen grown men break their bats over their legs and words come out of their mouth that was shocking to say the least. Instead of taking responsibility for their play, they start developing a poor attitude, sulk, and make excuses for the outcomes. This leads them down a dangerous and destructive path of no return. This rubs off on the other players and soon it's noticeable that you're on a losing team.

Life can send us many opportunities and we have to discover when those opportunities are either building us up or breaking us down. We have to sometimes cut the ties of the past and move on to new avenues that will open new doors. Those doors can lead you to develop positive relationships, better employment, or an even a much more satisfying life. The batter within a losing team has to be determined to seek a change by looking deep down within him or herself to realize their true worth. Seeking personal growth and new opportunities is no easy task. The first issue that a person must face is their fears. Fear can paralyze people into staying in a poor relationship, job, or any life situation. Fear can rob people of discovering new joys, and what can lie ahead waiting for them when they face them. Facing those fears takes courage, commitment, and a plan. The most important aspect of facing fears, is to surround yourself with positive people who can support you through the ups and downs. Surrounding yourself with people who truly care, can make a difference between success and failure. Many batters end up surrounding themselves with people who want the high life without any thought of what lies ahead. They are so caught up in the game that they forget about the days when hard times come. They end up hitting a wall of disappointment, regret, and sorrow. These batters forget about staying focused, balanced, and with right people. The people who love them the most will always support them through the wins and loses. Those special people are what keep them grounded and secure. Surrounding yourself with positive influences can help you realize when you're on a losing team. They can assist with the transition to move

Knowing When You're On A Losing Team

you in the right direction and to a new team that will be the best fit. Discovering the winning team may take some time to find, but staying on the wrong team may only destroy any chance of ever finding victory! Never stay with toxic people who destroy your chance, pick people who love you and will support you all the way until the end. Nobody wants to be on a losing team, but everyone wants to be a part of the joy on a winning team. It is a matter of a choice, pick one and the right people to get you there!

Pressing On but Live in the Moment

Philippians 3:14 NIV "I press on toward the goal to win the prize for which God has called me heavenward in Christ Jesus."

There are times in life we need to press on. We can't look back or worry about what is going to come our way. We have to stay the course and focus on the ride. Many baseball players try to worry about their bad plays, what happened in last night's game, or so many unresolved issues that stop them from moving forward. They also focus too often on their destiny, self-worth, prestige in the league, without a true sense of what is going on at the moment. They miss out on the opportunity to enjoy the moments, build relationships, or be more than they can be to themselves, and others around them. It is all about the game or is there so much more to live for? They become frustrated when things don't go their way but, pay too little attention to what is going on around them. They become disgruntled, disrespectful, and don't own their part in the game. Others may focus too much attention on the title, position, and monetary opportunity that they believe is due. Many times, those aspirations don't always come true, with an injury or any setback that leaves them struggling in developing to their full potential. Looking back and focusing too much on what is to come leaves out a huge gap in what they are doing in the present. They forget about the other players, the coaches, and all the people who are there with them during each game. They forget to laugh, enjoy, or take pride in their accomplishments they made during the game. They need to press on from each moment and enjoy the ride while it last.

Life can be the same for so many people. They get stuck in time with their dreams and aspirations, because of what happened in the past or they focus too much about what and where they want to be. Maybe it's the fear of what has happened in the past keeps them from moving forward. They don't know how to deal with past problems so this haunts them each day from developing to their full potential. Past problems can create a barrier to present satisfaction in life. Many people repeat the same mistakes and find they are in an even deeper hole. Instead of dealing with the problems of the past, they avoid or ignore the signs that tell them that something within themselves is missing or left unfinished. This unfinished business seems to cloud their minds and slows them from progressing further.

Pressing On But Live In The Moment

While others seem to focus so hard on what they want, they plow over anything or anyone in their way. They become disinterested in any signs to slow them down or to take a detour. Either way, both kinds of people forget about the present and to press on from there. Living in the moment does not mean to forget the past or worry about the future. It is about realizing where you came from and setting realistic goals to where you want to go. It is about having a plan of attack, while enjoying the ride. We have to understand that the past does not have to define us, but we learn from the past. We learn to do things better, become stronger, develop confidence, courage, and the conviction to move on. We may need professional help, help from friends, family, or our church to get through the issues of the past that haunt us. Those issues can create barriers that scar us for life. You cannot let those past issues stop you from moving forward. You have to define who you are and who you want to be in life. Yes, bad things do happen to all of us, but it's your choices that surround those issues is what makes a difference in becoming a victim or victor. The past is over, but we often want to live in the past because the future looks to scary to face. With the help of others is what will pull you through it. Live each day for what it gives you, to the best of your ability. Tomorrow is not always promised. We all have dreams, aspirations, and goals. Live life with the heart of facing each challenge as it comes, as a victor not a victim. Chose great people to surround you. Keep your eyes focused on your heart's desires but, don't lose sight of what is going

Losing is NOT an Option

on around you too. Don't give in, give up, or bail out. Press on each day, no matter what life throws at you. Dig down deep in yourself and know you can beat what comes your way with a well thought out plan of action. You are way too smart to let life's problems drag you down. Get back up when life pushes you down. God created you in His perfect image. He will help you along the way. Press on and know that you too will get through this and come out the other side swinging like a pro!

The Game is Not Over

1 Corinthians 9:24 NIV "Do you not know that in a race all the runners run, but only one receives the prize? So run that you may obtain it."

Every season comes to an end, but it doesn't mean the game is over. "There is a time for everything, and a season for every activity under heavens: a time to be born and a time to die, a time to plant and a time to uproot, a time to kill and a time to heal, a time to tear down and a time to build, a time to weep, and a time to laugh, a time to mourn and a time to dance, a time to scatter stones and a time to gather them, a time to embrace and a time to refrain from embracing, a time to search and a time to give up, a time to keep and a time to throw away, a time to tear and a time to mend, a time to be silent and a time to speak, a time to love and a time to hate, a time for war and a time for peace... He has made everything beautiful in its time" Ecclesiastes 3:1 NIV

I read this and it reminds me of the entire season of baseball and life. We have so much time to enjoy and experience the game and life to fullness. Except, with that experience, comes challenges that may rock the foundation and change the way we look at things. The game teaches us so much about life, with how we come to terms with everything. It teaches us about the battles, victories, and even defeats. These are all life lessons that so many people struggle with and not everyone has the ability to face the challenges or deal with what happens on and off the field. These people may not have the skills, resources, or aptitude to face difficult situations or challenges in their lives. They bail out and find dysfunctional ways of coping with challenges. This can lead them down a dangerous and destructive path that eventually rocks their world, along with the people they love. They make poor choices that can result in loss of relationships, jobs, and even of self. They struggle, trying to find their way through life, because they do not realize the impact it has on themselves and their future outcomes. Many of these people find themselves in a deep hole that they just don't have the ability to climb out of. Eventually, they either sink or rise to the occasion. Whereas others seem to coast along, knowing and understanding the obstacles in life and face them one by one. They accept that life is not always perfect and deal with the reality of difficult times with the right attitude, by making the right choices, and with the love and support of others. These people get through life without falling apart when things go wrong. They become even stronger as they face each challenge and learn from their mistakes, rather than wallow in them. They are not victims, but victors as they learn to rely on their internal strengths in facing what lies ahead. They develop character, confidence, and conviction to be all they can be, to make this world a better place, and to uplift the people around them with what they do. They contribute, not contaminate, this world because they have learned what it takes to conquer problems, find solutions, and determine outcomes that best support their goals. This can be applied to the game of baseball too. There are many types of players and how they deal with the ups and down of the game, eventually effects the final score. Players understand the hardships that come with playing the game. They also understand that hard work, dedication, and perseverance is what separates the winners from the losers. It seems so clear what it takes to succeed, but not everyone has the vision to see this so clearly. Some may take time to wake up to the fact that life has its challenges and it takes an inner strength, positive attitude, and a supportive network to overcome them. While others understand exactly what it takes to preserve and overcome these challenges that result in success.

    Life can be simple as a baseball game, but not everyone will see it that way. They continue down the same path of drama, recklessness, and destruction. They live for the moment and don't see the consequences of their actions. They harbor anger, resentment, and become victims to the choices they have created. While others walk up to the plate with an understanding of what it will take to win. They have so much determination to hit that ball out of the park and are willing to do what it takes to succeed. In the end, it is a matter of attitude and choice. The game is not easy, it will always send you a curve ball, but it is up to you to "keep your head in the game." Now go play ball, the game is not over yet, it's just begun!

The Season is Over

Isaiah 40:31 New International Version (NIV)
"³¹ but those who hope in the Lord
will renew their strength.
They will soar on wings like eagles;
they will run and not grow weary,
they will walk and not be faint."

The season is over, as the last game was played. The batter looks at the score board for one last time. He remembers the highlights of the many games played and walks off the field with an empty feeling. The season was filled with sparks of emotional highs and lows, wins and losses, and many memories of a game played with passion. The batter put in so much personal time, energy, and skills to assist the team throughout the year. Each time a game was played, it brought a new desire to take it to the next level. The goal is to be the best he can be, on the team for the ultimate trophy at the end. Whether the trophy was won or not, does not signify the personal commitment each player gave to the team. Life does not always turn out the way we want and we must face many battles. We work hard to accomplish our dreams and goals but it comes with many sacrifices and giving your personal best. There are times when life takes us down a path of great successes and often follows by huge failures. We look at the season with awe and wonder why those losses happen. We blame ourselves, become angry, and at times, turn into a victim of despair. Hopelessness is a choice when a person sees no future for them. The famous saying to "keep your head in the game" is so true at this point in the journey. Losses do happen during the season but having a plan, a new approach, and a commitment to the game is what changes hopelessness into a new life in the game. Each game and every season is a brand new opportunity to reinvest in yourself, to be the best and accomplish your dreams. Looking back on the season, gives each player a perspective of the game. Reflecting back can be a positive or negative venture. Reflecting on the past can take you down into despair, if one does not face reality. Reality knows that you did your absolute best, you gave it your all, and you are ready to face the next season with a new attitude and approach. Ending the season on that note is what most professional players do. However, there are those who look back with gloom and doom. They focus on every negative play, blame their team mates for their

The Season Is Over

failures, and wallow in despair. They end the season depressed and with no excitement or hopes of future events. They don't look deep inside themselves to see where they failed and how they can challenge themselves to do better. While there are also some players who end the season with a positive attitude and belief that win or lose, they knew they gave it their all. They look back with knowing that the game was rough, not everything always turned out exactly as they expected, and they are willing to give even more next season. The season is over to give us an opportunity to recap, regroup, and regain a winning plan for the next one to come. The season may be over, but each batter knows that training for the next game never ends. In life, you always have to be willing and ready to face every opportunity with a new approach for what is in store for you. Don't lost heart or hope, don't give up, and "keep your head in the game." Hopefully, you will value and cherish that special person, players, or coach by your side to get you to the next season. Last, remember personally acknowledge them for sticking it out with you and their willingness to take you on next year. It takes a great person to put up with each player's temperament, flaws, and yet still see the best in them. Don't ever forget the one who led you to the season's end. The season may be over for some, but to others, it's just another step in life that has just begun.

Saying Goodbye

Jeremiah 29 NIV "'¹ For I know the plans I have for you,' declares the LORD, 'plans to prosper you and not to harm you, plans to give you hope and a future. ¹² Then you will call on me and come and pray to me, and I will listen to you. ¹³ You will seek me and find me when you seek me with all your heart.'"

Saying goodbye at the end of the season is probably the hardest thing to do in the game. Each player dedicated their time, energy, and skills to the team for a successful season. The bonding that occurred as a result of playing together holds the hearts of each player for a lifetime. The team shared so many memories, experiences, along with the ups and downs of the game. Although the time was limited, each player will look back at the season with awe and wonder why it ever ended so quickly. Nobody wants to say goodbye, and everyone wants the game to continue forever, but it just doesn't. The learning that followed with each game, the trust that was developed, and the personal growth should not be taken ever so lightly. The game created moments of excitement, challenges, and often, followed by failures. These moments do not discount the love that grew with facing those challenges and making it through each game in an effort to face the next opportunity to do it even better. The love for the game, the love for each player, and the love for the time is what will always stay in the heart. Developing a bonding friendship with people is no easy task, when so many personalities on a team exist. The friendships in life that do develop are special and are a result of two people who have a common interest, passion, and value for each other's time. The time spent with that friend is what gets you through may difficult days and can assist you to focus on the positives instead of the negatives. Friendship does not develop without flaws. But comes with tempers, tears, and hard work. It takes two people willing to come together with an understanding and define where the friendship will take them. Friendship is strengthened when it is followed with a commitment to develop a meaningful relationship based upon trust, honesty, and mutual respect. There is no other highlight in life than developing a best friend and to share so many powerful experiences together. Friendships can last a life time if nurtured and valued by each other. The game will go on next season, but not all the players will be back. The friendships developed

Saying Goodbye

along the way is what carries you to the next season, while still hoping that special person will still be there along your side rooting for you all the way to the end. Saying goodbye can only be for a brief period of time in the game until you all come together again. The life lesson is to learn to hold on to that special friend you made during the season and remember that true friends will always stay close by your side and close to your heart. Don't ever lose a true friend, because they are worth more than the season's trophy or any weight in gold. Only a fool will discount the worth of a true friend, but a wise person will do what it takes to keep that special person in his or her life. You may have to say goodbye to some people in your life for now, but never say goodbye to that true friend. Life is way too short not to be surrounded by the people who love you the most. Cherish that special friend and don't ever lose one who is willing to stand by your side. Saying goodbye doesn't mean it's all over but it may also mean it's just begun.

Starting Over

Numbers 6:24-26 NIV "The LORD bless you and keep you; the LORD make his face shine on you and be gracious to you; the LORD turn his face toward you and give you peace."

Starting over after the season ends comes with making some hard decisions. Each player has to pick up the pieces where they left off. A saddened feeling overwhelms the process because of the emotional roller coaster faced during the season. The ups and downs of the games, wins and losses, and personal challenges faced along the way create an uneasiness to know what lies ahead. The sadness comes from the letdown after it all comes to a screeching halt. The season was filled with so much excitement and the thought of it all being over can create a deep depression if each player does not look forward to what lies ahead. Looking back at all the memories is a healthy step in the process, but fixating on it can only keep you stuck from moving forward. The season was special with giving your personal best, achieving all of your goals, meeting so many wonderful people, and enjoying the game. Starting over is the next step when the season is over and you said your goodbyes. Starting over doesn't mean you lose anything along the way. You learn just how much you've accomplished, how many people you met, and how much more you can do.

Life can take you through many seasons and each season can assist you to face the next one with growing in courage, confidence, and character. Relationships end, jobs end, people move, and many other changes occur during life. Life does not stay stagnant but, moves people to new opportunities and positions that force them to start over again. Starting over is no easy task and relies on planning, preparation, and hard work. Each person has to plan a new strategy, prepare for the changes, and work diligently to accomplish the new goals desired. Starting over may take some time so patience is a necessity. Rushing through the process can only create more difficulties along the way. Maintaining a positive attitude will also assist in creating a smooth transition to the process. Some people do not do well with changes and do it kicking and screaming until they are forced to make the necessary adjustments. Other people face changes with a willing spirit and an attitude of opportunity and growth. The latter choice can assist you with opening new doors of opportunities that lie ahead. Sometimes, what lies

Starting Over

beyond those doors can lead you to even more positive experiences and happiness. The window of opportunity relies on the willingness to take that risk to start all over again. Some people bail out at this most difficult moment in life, only to sit on the sidelines. Others walk through the door with courage and confidence to face any new opportunities presented. What lies ahead can create a whole new world filled with endless adventures and lead you to your created destiny. The pain faced with starting all over again can be lessoned when you are surrounded by people who love and support you during such times. Embrace them and give them a chance to assist you with that transition. Take them with you and show them what you are made of. In the end, you will prove that it was not that bad after all. You may even come out a whole lot stronger and excited. Soon a whole new season will start again, and you have to be ready to play each game with a new attitude and approach to the plate. Except, what you have learned along the way, while surrounded by the people you love the most, will assist you to do it all over again, to be your personal best. Face every opportunity to start all over with knowing that you will succeed and come out a better person in the end!

Never Stop Fighting...
Losing Is Not an Option...
Keep Your Head in the Game

It's been over ten years now and a lot has happened since my son started baseball. He's moved up from Little League, to High School, along with travel baseball. Baseball is his passion, but was a humbling experience over the years, but the lessons learned will last him a lifetime. He's currently playing at the college level, which is a whole new ball game. He's developed character, confidence and a conviction to continue to give it all that he has. Just like you realize in life things are not always fair, you have to take a few bumps and bruises along the way. You have to swallow your pride, tough it out, and even learn to get along with some difficult people. There are times he was able to shine and there were times of struggling to prove his worth. He continued to play his game, no matter the circumstances. He believed in what he was doing was worth the effort or he would have quit a long time ago. He not only learned to develop physically, with weight training, but mentally, with understanding situational playing. You cannot play the game without knowing what pitch to throw, where to be during the play, how to be crafty and deceiving with your delivery, and how to dominate the mound, even when the best batter is at the plate. He loves the game and even though he's never going to the major leagues, he will always have the memories of the game, friends, and will graduate with a degree in Chemical Engineering when it's all over. See, he realizes his limitations, but never allowed anything to keep him from his desire to play the game. There will always be players better than you and some will quit along the way, but no matter where you are in the mix, you have to keep your head in the game. I'm very proud of him for not giving up and continuing the battle to make his dreams come true. Who would have ever thought that he could eventually play at the college level, especially with showing up at his first practice with a vinyl glove and cheap bat from Meijer's. He just felt something inside of him to continue playing, no matter what any other player, coach, or umpire said to discourage him. He kept his head up and battled through each season. He was determined to get better through many challenging games, teams, and seasons. He didn't allow himself to feel unworthy to play so he learned, practiced, conditioned, and did whatever it took to get better. He was no big kid and wasn't gifted athletically but with passion, hard work, and a brain, he was able to become a starting pitcher and a very good one. We spent a lot of time traveling to different

Never Stop Fighting…losing Is Not An Option…keep Your Head In The Game

tournaments but, enjoyed each step of the way with team. We were able to enjoy a vacation in Myrtle Beach South Carolina for the Cal Ripken tournament. Now that was a most worthy trip to take but, it was hot. I remember he pitched a game where he got heat stroke because the coach lost track of the number of pitches he threw, but he battled through it. He pitched in the extreme cold, rain, and heat throughout the years, as if it was just another game without complaining. Fortunately, he never got seriously injured throughout the years but, he did have to play with a sprained wrist for a season in high school, which messed up his batting average. That's life, you have to take the bumps and bruises and press on. Much of any sport is having mental toughness and being able to handle difficult situations. If you can't take the heat, then you might as well sit the bench or don't play at all. My son was able to take a lot of things but, it helped him to develop as a man. He has learned to take responsibility for his actions, temper his emotions, and think of what's best for the team more than himself. These are honorable character traits that will help him in life with making good decisions. Future employers will understand the nature of an athlete, their drive, competitive spirit, willingness to do more, team approach, flexibility, resourcefulness, ability to learn and challenge themselves to be the best. Leadership skills are hard to find in many young college students who have no job experience but, being part of a team puts him ahead of many with nothing on their resume. He will take all he has learned, achieved, and valued throughout his life, so when he finds new challenges, he will be able to handle them. It's great to see him on the mound at the college level. I just look back and remember the journey. It was filled with great memories, friendships, fears, frustrations, tears, and great joy. The most important thing he will always have, is knowing he never gave in to his fears, battled each obstacle along the way, and continued to be the best person and player he could possibly be.

Life is just like that, in everything you do. It's not always easy and it could bring you to your knees, but you can never give up hope. Hope is something you believe in when everything or everyone else says you can't. There is no can't in hope because it allows you to see past your limitations, failures, fears, anxieties, and obstacles. Hope is what makes people accomplish their desired dreams and aspirations. When people lose hope, they make poor choices and life takes them farther away from everything they desire. This doesn't mean it's going to happen overnight, nor without struggles and it could even come with failure. Except, without hope you will just sit on the bench in life as the seasons pass you by. Hopelessness will make you not try, bail out, or even give up, but when you turn it around in your head, you can make things happen. This starts with a plan, vision, and time table. You have to have realistic goals but, map out how you're going to get there. You may need to get help along the way but, asking for help is not a bad thing. The most successful people have had help, sometimes you just can't do it by yourself. You need people to hold you accountable or you may wonder off course with distractions. That is

Never Stop Fighting...losing Is Not An Option...keep Your Head In The Game

what is so great about the team atmosphere; you have plenty of coaches and peers to keep you on your toes. You know if you slack off even a little bit, you're going to be a bench player. This can be applied to many circumstances in life, because true friends will be honest with you. They will tell you when you're not pulling your weight or going in the wrong direction. It's up to you to listen and pride is not going to help you develop. Pride is a road block to anything you seek to obtain. It creates a selfish, self-centered, and self-righteous person who isn't willing to evaluate themselves. You have to be able to look in the mirror and like what you see. When you are prideful is distorts who you are and what you see and it affects what you do and how you do it. When you are realistic with your strengths and weaknesses, you're able to improve on the weaknesses and build on your strengths. The most important lesson, is to always be willing to learn more, do more, and give more of yourself. Eventually you will see small successes and build in the process that will bring you to your desired destination. Success is the end result and each person will have to know what that means to them as an individual. Each person comes with values, cultures, beliefs, and ideals that will be opened up to endless possibilities in the end. Your future depends on what you do, how you do it, and your attitude along the way. Keep your head in the game means you never stop fighting for what you believe in, you never stop moving forward, and you never stop believing in who you are or what you want to accomplish. For it's the never quitting, hoping, and believing you can do it is what makes dreams come true. If you truly want things to happen, then you have to be willing to go the distance, you have to overcome obstacles, and you give it all that you have. Then you can say I did it, I made a difference, not only to me, but to all those around me. For the game of life is never over until your heart stops beating, you take that last breath, and they turn off the stadium lights. Baseball is a life long journey but, you will never be disappointed as long as you "keep your head in the game." The most important life lessons you can get from this book is no matter how many times you get knocked down, get hurt, fall apart, or even fail, it's not over. Life will hit you hard, but you have to be resilient to get back up to the plate, and swing that bat again and again. Losing Is Not an Option, it's a choice, now go and make the right one! God Bless You!

CPSIA information can be obtained
at www.ICGtesting.com
Printed in the USA
FSHW010721060819